D1565927

COMMERCIAL LAW

by

Margaret C. Jasper, Esq.

Oceana's Legal Almanac Series:
Law for the Layperson

1998
Oceana Publications, Inc.
Dobbs Ferry, N.Y.

In rmation contained in this work has been obtained by Oceana Publications fr 1 sources believed to be reliable. However, neither the Publisher nor its au ors guarantee the accuracy or completeness of any information published he in, and neither Oceana nor its authors shall be responsible for any errors, om ssions or damages arising from the use of this information. This work is put ished with the understanding that Oceana and its authors are supplying informa-tio , but are not attempting to render legal or other professional services. If such ser ices are required, the assistance of an appropriate professional should be sought.

Library of Congress Cataloging-in-Publication Data

Jasper, Margaret C.
    Commercial law / by Margaret C. Jasper.
        p. cm.—(Oceana's legal almanac series. Law for the layperson)
    Includes bibliographical references.
    ISBN 0-379-11326-0 (acid-free paper)
    1. Business law—United States. I. Title. II. Series.
KF889.6.J37 1998   98-48862
346.7307—dc21   CIP

Oceana's Legal Almanac Series: Law for the Layperson
ISSN: 1075-7376

To My Husband Chris

Your love and support
are my motivation and inspiration

-and-

In memory of my son, Jimmy

ABOUT THE AUTHOR

MARGARET C. JASPER is an attorney engaged in the general practice of law in South Salem, New York, concentrating in the areas of personal injury and entertainment law. Ms. Jasper holds a Juris Doctor degree from Pace University School of Law, White Plains, New York, is a member of the New York and Connecticut bars, and is certified to practice before the United States District Courts for the Southern and Eastern Districts of New York, and the United States Supreme Court.

Ms. Jasper has been appointed to the panel of arbitrators of the American Arbitration Association and the law guardian panel for the Family Court of the State of New York, is a member of the Association of Trial Lawyers of America, and is a New York State licensed real estate broker and member of the Westchester County Board of Realtors, operating as Jasper Real Estate, in South Salem, New York.

Ms. Jasper is the author and general editor of the following legal almanacs: Juvenile Justice and Children's Law; Marriage and Divorce; Estate Planning; The Law of Contracts; The Law of Dispute Resolution; Law for the Small Business Owner; The Law of Personal Injury; Real Estate Law for the Homeowner and Broker; Everyday Legal Forms; Dictionary of Selected Legal Terms; The Law of Medical Malpractice; The Law of Product Liability; The Law of No-Fault Insurance; The Law of Immigration; The Law of Libel and Slander; The Law of Buying and Selling; Elder Law; The Right to Die; AIDS Law; The Law of Obscenity and Pornography; The Law of Child Custody; The Law of Debt Collection; Consumer Rights Law; Bankruptcy Law for the Individual Debtor; Victim's Rights Law; Animal Rights Law; Workers' Compensation Law; Employee Rights in theWorkplace; Probate Law; Environmental Law; Labor Law; The Americans with Disabilities Act; The Law of Capital Punishment; Education Law; The Law of Violence Against Women; Landlord-Tenant Law; Insurance Law; and Religion and the Law.

TABLE OF CONTENTS

INTRODUCTION

Commercial law governs the broad areas of business, commerce, and consumer transactions. Specific law has developed in a number of commercial fields, and has been codified in a number of statutes. The Uniform Commercial Code (UCC) is the primary source of commercial law in the United States.

The UCC refers to the set of laws drafted by the National Conference of Commissioners on Uniform State Laws (NCCUSL), in an attempt to promote certainty and predictability in the area of commercial law in order to facilitate commercial transactions. It was intended that such a comprehensive law would reduce the number of legal disputes arising out of commercial matters. Additions or revisions to the UCC are proposed by the NCCUSL and the American Law Institute (ALI).

The NCCUSL recognized that it would be particularly advantageous if the UCC were uniformly adopted by all of the states with little or no revision or amendment. Although all of the states have adopted some form of the UCC, they have included a number of jurisdictional amendments. The UCC has not been enacted as federal law, however, it is the governing law in the District of Columbia. The UCC provisions become the governing law in those jurisdictions which adopt its provisions, in whole or in part.

This legal almanac explores the law of commercial transactions as governed by the UCC. Although it would be impossible to give an in-depth analysis of such a comprehensive statute as the UCC in such limited space, this almanac offers an overview of each Article, and highlights general principles and important provisions.

The UCC is divided into thirteen separate Articles:

Article 1: General Provisions

Article 2: Sales

Article 2A: Leases

Article 3: Commercial Paper

Article 4: Bank Deposits and Collections

Article 4A. Funds Transfers

Article 5: Letters of Credit

Article 6: Bulk Sales

Article 7: Warehouse Receipts, Bills of Lading and Other Documents of Title

Article 8: Investment Securities

Article 9: Secured Transactions; Sales of Accounts and Chattel Paper

Article 10: Effective Date and Repealer

Article 11: Effective Date and Transition Provisions

This almanac examines Articles 2 through 9, which set forth the substantive topics addressed by the UCC. In addition, this almanac also discusses the proposed Article 2B: Licensing, which is presently being drafted by the NCCUSL and the American Law Institute (ALI).

This almanac intends to give the reader a general understanding of the primary law governing commercial transactions. The UCC does not address every aspect of commercial law. There are certain purportedly commercial matters which are not addressed by the UCC, such as the sale of real property, insurance contracts, bankruptcy matters, and suretyship transactions. Such matters are left to the jurisdiction of general contract law.

In addition, certain topics which are covered by the UCC must still rely on non-UCC law for support, guidance and clarification. In addition, where there is a federal law which conflicts with a UCC provision, the federal law will prevail over the UCC.

The Appendix provides applicable sections of the UCC as cited throughout the almanac, and other pertinent information and data. The Glossary contains definitions of terms used in commercial law, as well as many of the UCC terms used throughout the almanac.

CHAPTER 1:

UCC ARTICLE 2 - SALES

In General

Most transactions involving the sale of goods are governed by state law. Article 2 regulates every phase of a transaction for the sale of goods and provides remedies for problems that may arise.

The UCC defines *goods* as "all things which are movable and identified to the contract of the sale." To be "identified to the contract," a "good" must be existing, and one of the objects that is or will be exchanged between merchants and consumers.

See UCC Sections 2-105 at Appendix 1.

Federal law has a limited impact on transactions for the sale of goods. The Bankruptcy Code, Title 11 §§ 2 and 9, regulates claims that may arise from sales transactions in a bankruptcy case. The Magnuson-Moss Warranty Act, 5 U.S.C. § 2301, regulates explicit and implied warranties, and the Consumer Credit Protection Act, 15 U.S.C. § 1667, provides protection to consumers entering into leases.

The Statute of Frauds

Article 2 requires that there be some writing sufficient to indicate that a contract for the sale of goods was entered into by the parties, and signed by the party against whom enforcement is sought. The statute applies to the sale of goods with a value of $500 or over. The writing must recite a quantity term. If such a writing is produced, the contract may be enforced, but only for the quantity of goods shown in the writing.

Notwithstanding the foregoing requirements pertaining to the sufficiency of the writing, the UCC also states that a written confirmation between merchants, which is signed by the sender, and which recites a quantity term, need not be signed by the party to be charged in order to be enforceable. If the receiving party does not want the goods, it is incumbent upon him to send a written notice of objection to the Seller within 10 days after the written confirmation is received.

Exceptions

If the contract does not satisfy the writing requirement, it may still be valid and enforceable under the following conditions:

1. If the goods are specially manufactured for the Buyer and the Seller has substantially begun production or procurement of the goods prior to receiving a notice of repudiation from the Buyer; or

2. If the party who is being charged makes an admission in court, by pleadings, testimony or otherwise, that a contract for sale was made; or

3. If the goods have been received and accepted, or if payment for the goods has been made and accepted.

See UCC Section 2-201 at Appendix 1.

The Parol Evidence Rule

Under the UCC, the terms of a final written agreement, or confirmatory memoranda between the parties, may not be contradicted by evidence of any prior agreement or contemporaneous oral agreement.

See UCC Section 2-202 at Appendix 1.

Exceptions

The UCC does allow the parties to explain or supplement the writing by introducing evidence involving:

1. Course of Dealing - Course of dealing refers to the sequence of previous conduct between the parties to a particular transaction which is fairly to be regarded as establishing a common basis of understanding for interpreting their expressions and other conduct.

2. Usage of Trade - Usage of trade refers to any practice or method of dealing having such regularity of observance in a place, vocation or trade as to justify an expectation that it will be observed with respect to the transaction in question.

3. Course of Performance - Course of performance shall be relevant where the contract for sale involves repeated occasions for performance by either party with knowledge of the nature of the performance and opportunity for objection to it by the other, where such course of performance was accepted or acquiesced in without objection.

See UCC Section 2-205 at Appendix 1.

Duty of Good Faith and Fair Dealing

Under the UCC, every contract imposes upon each party a duty of good faith and fair dealing in its performance and its enforcement. The UCC defines *good faith* as "honesty in fact in the conduct or transaction concerned." In the case of a merchant, the UCC provides that good faith means "honesty in fact and the observance of reasonable commercial standards of fair dealing in the trade."

Contract Formation

Under Article 2, a contract for the sale of goods may be made in any manner sufficient to show that an agreement was reached by the parties. This is so even if the exact time the agreement was reached is indefinite. Further, the contract will still be found valid even if one or more terms are missing, provided the parties intended to make the contract, and there is a reasonably certain basis for furnishing an appropriate remedy.

See UCC Section 2-204 at Appendix 1.

Offer and Acceptance

Offer

Under Article 2, in order to be a valid offer, a contract generally need only provide the quantity of items to be sold. An exception exists when a contract for the sale of goods calls for the Buyer's purchase of the "total output" of the Seller—known as an "output" contract—or when the contract calls for the Buyer's promise to purchase all the product that Buyer "requires" from the Seller—known as a "requirements" contract.

In that case, a "reasonable" quantity will be implied by the Court should there be a dispute. If there has been a stated estimate, the Court may use this as a guideline to determine a good faith quantity. If there is no stated estimate, the Court may consider the terms of prior output contracts between the parties.

See UCC Section 2-301 and 2-306 at Appendix 1.

Merchant's Firm Offer

A merchant's firm offer is defined as an offer by a merchant to buy or sell goods, in a signed writing which, by its terms, gives assurance that it will be held open. If the assurance is supplied by the offeree, the writing must also be signed by the offeror in order to make it a binding firm offer.

The merchant's firm offer is not revocable during the time stated in the writing. However, if there is no time stated in the writing, the offer will be deemed irrevocable for a reasonable period of time. In either case, despite what the writing may state, the period of irrevocability may not exceed three months.

Unlike an option contract, which requires that the offeree give some consideration to hold an offer open for a stated period of time, the merchant's firm offer under the UCC does not require any consideration.

See UCC Section 2-205 at Appendix 1.

Counter-Offers

The UCC sets forth various rules concerning counter-offers in connection with the sale of goods. Counter-offers are limited to the following two methods:

1. By shipping non-conforming goods as an accommodation; or

2. By making words of acceptance expressly conditioned on a new or different term.

Irrevocable Offers

There are certain offers which cannot be terminated and thus deemed irrevocable, as follows:

1. Merchant's Firm Offer - Generally, if a merchant puts an offer in writing stating that it will be held open, that offer is irrevocable for the time stated in the writing, or for a reasonable amount of time if the writing is silent as to the time period. A reasonable amount of time is generally deemed to be no more than 3 months unless consideration has been paid to the merchant to extend the time period.

2. Option Contract - Generally, if consideration is received by the offeror to keep the offer open for an agreed period of time, the offer is irrevocable for that period of time and is the subject matter of the option contract. In addition, if the offeree detrimentally, reasonably and foreseeably relies on the offer, this may be deemed a substitute for the required consideration.

3. Unilateral Contract Offers - Generally, offers to make unilateral contracts—contracts in which the offeror warns the offeree that the only way the offeree can accept is by completing performance—are irrevocable for a period of time.

Acceptance

An offer to make a contract must be construed as inviting acceptance in any manner and by any medium deemed reasonable under the circumstances, unless otherwise unambiguously indicated by the language or the circumstances. Under the UCC, the offer contained in a contract involving the sale of goods is generally accepted by either (1) a promise to buy goods, or (2) by performance.

In addition, there are certain rules which accompany acceptance by performance, as follows:

(a) If performance will take some time, then notice that the performance will take place is required;

(b) Acceptance occurs whether performance consisted of shipping the right goods or the wrong goods. The rationale for this is that we must make the shipment an acceptance of the offer so that there is a valid contract which can be declared to have been breached in order to provide the Buyer with a remedy at law against the Seller of the non-conforming goods.

Nevertheless, an exception to this rule exists when the Seller states that the shipment of non-conforming goods is being sent as an accommodation to the Buyer. In this case, the shipment of non-conforming goods is treated as a counter-offer which may or may not be accepted by the Buyer.

The counter-offer, as set forth above, in effect rejects the original offer. If the Buyer uses the non-conforming goods, he is deemed to have accepted the counter-offer and thus a contract is formed.

Nevertheless, where the beginning of the requested performance is a reasonable method of acceptance, an offeror who has not been notified of acceptance within a reasonable time may treat the offer as having lapsed before acceptance.

See UCC Section 2-206 at Appendix 1.

Modification

Modifications to a contract need not be accompanied by consideration to be enforceable. However, if the contract does not permit modification or rescission unless it is in a signed writing, the modification would not be enforceable without such writing. Nevertheless, any form supplied by a merchant for this purpose must also be signed by the other party, unless the agreement is made between merchants.

Consideration

Consideration is the inducement to enter into a contract. Consideration may involve some right, interest, profit, or benefit which accrues to one party, or some forbearance, detriment, loss or responsibility undertaken by the other party. Simply stated, the consideration is what each party bargains for in the agreement. The court generally does not concern itself with the fairness or adequacy of the consideration. However, on occasion, if the consideration appears patently unfair or grossly inadequate, the court may rule that the contract is unenforceable due to unconscionability.

Unconscionability

Unconscionability refers to an absence of meaningful choice on the part of one of the contracting parties, together with contract terms which are unreasonably favorable to the other contracting party. A determination that a contract or term is unconscionable is made by the court in light of all the material facts. Under the UCC, the determination is made "as a matter of law."

The UCC states that a contract may not be enforced if the court finds the contract, or any clause of the contract, to have been unconscionable at the time it was made. The court has the option of enforcing the remainder of the contract without the unconscionable clause, or placing a limitation on the unconscionable clause to avoid an unconscionable result from its application. The parties to the contract are permitted to introduce evidence as to commercial setting, purpose and effect, to show that the contract, or a clause of the contract, is not unconscionable and aid the court in its determination.

See UCC Section 2-302 at Appendix 1.

Warranties

There are three basic types of warranties upon which a Buyer relies: (1) Express Warranty; (2) Implied Warranty of Merchantability; and (3) Implied Warranty of Fitness for a Particular Purpose.

Express Warranty

Under the UCC, an express warranty is any affirmation of fact, description or sample furnished by the Seller to the Buyer that relates to the goods and becomes part of the basis of the bargain. Thus, it is expressly warranted that the product will conform to such affirmation, description or sample.

Further, it is not necessary that the warranty be reduced to writing, nor that any particular words be used, such as "guarantee," in order to create the obligation, as long as the representations were meant to be factual and not mere opinion.

See UCC Section 2-313 at Appendix 1.

Implied Warranty of Merchantability

An implied warranty of merchantability is an implied representation that the product is free of defects and meets the general standards of acceptability. Under the UCC, a warranty of merchantability is implied in a contract of sale if the seller is considered a merchant in goods of that type, unless the implied warranty is excluded or modified. Under this section, merchantable goods are those which:

1. Pass without objection in the trade;

2. Are of fair average quality;

3. Are fit for the ordinary purposes for which such goods are used;

4. Are of uniform kind, quality, and quantity within each unit or shipment;

5. Are adequately contained, packaged, and labeled; and

6. Conform to any express warranty given on the container or label.

See UCC Section 2-314 at Appendix 1.

Implied Warranty of Fitness for a Particular Purpose

As the name demonstrates, this warranty includes the obligation that the product meets the Buyer's needs for a particular purpose. Thus, although a product may be merchantable, it still may be a breach of the implied warranty of fitness for a particular purpose.

See UCC Section 2-315 at Appendix 1.

Risk of Loss

Risk of loss refers to the set of rules that govern in determining the party liable for goods involved in a sale should they be damaged or lost at some point during the transfer from Seller to Buyer. In general, risk of loss passes from the Seller to the Buyer when the Seller has completed performance under the contract, as follows:

Face-to-Face Delivery

If the Seller is a merchant, the risk of loss passes upon physical receipt of the goods by the Buyer. However, if the Seller is not a merchant, then risk of loss occurs when tender of delivery occurs. For example, tender occurs when the Seller notifies the Buyer that the goods are available and makes the goods available to the Buyer.

Delivery by Intermediary or Carrier

The risk of loss depends on how the goods are shipped:

F.O.B.

F.O.B. refers to "free on board" to a stated destination, e.g. F.O.B. New York. This means that the goods will be priced so freight to the destination is included. If the goods are sent F.O.B. to a place other than where the Seller is—known as a *destination contract*—the Seller has an obligation to get the goods to the place and tender delivery by notice of availability and holding the goods for a reasonable time.

If the goods are damaged or lost either before they reach the destination, or before the goods are at the destination for a reasonable time, the duties are discharged. However, if the goods are at the destination for a reasonable time after Buyer is notified, and they are lost or damaged, it is the Buyer's problem and he must pay for the goods anyway.

F.A.S.

F.A.S. refers to "free along side" a particular port. This means that the price of the goods includes delivery to the port or ship.

C.I.F. and C. & F.

The term C.I.F. refers to "cost-insurance-freight to a particular Port. This means that the price includes in a lump sum the cost of the goods and the insurance and freight to the named destination.

The term C. & F. refers to "cost and freight" to a particular Port, and means that the price includes cost and freight to a particular destination.

For all of the above examples, except an FOB destination contract, the general risk of loss rule is that the risk of loss will pass when the Seller delivers the goods to the carrier and makes a reasonable contract for their delivery. This ends the Seller's responsibility.

See UCC Sections 2-319 and 2-320 at Appendix 1.

Casualty to Identified Goods

Casualty to identified goods—i.e., when goods are destroyed—operates to discharge the duties under the contract. The casualty must occur before the risk of loss has passed from Seller to Buyer. Identified goods are those which are either:

    1. Identified in the contract; or

2. Marked, shipped or otherwise designated as the goods under the contract.

If there is casualty before delivery of the goods to the carrier, then the duties are discharged. However, if there is casualty after delivery of the goods to the carrier, it is the Buyer's problem and he still must pay for the goods.

Where partial casualty of the shipment occurs, the Buyer has the option of either (1) treating the contract as terminated; or (2) electing to take the goods with a price adjustment.

Discharge of Duties Under Contract

A duty contained in a contract can be discharged in a number of ways, including but not limited to:

Modification

Modification occurs if the parties change their duties under the original contract. If a modification is enforceable, then the original duties are discharged and new duties arise.

Mutual Rescission/Cancellation/Release

A mutual rescission, cancellation or release of the duties contained in the contract eliminates the requirement of performance of those duties.

Accord and Satisfaction

Accord and satisfaction occurs when the parties to the original contract resolve a dispute existing in the contract and make a new agreement to satisfy the dispute. The accord, i.e., the new agreement, does not in itself eliminate the duties under the old contract. It is the satisfaction—the performance under the new agreement—that eliminates the duties under the old contract. If there is no satisfaction, i.e., performance of the accord, then a lawsuit can be brought to enforce the terms of the original contract.

Novation

A novation involves the substitution of a new party and new performance in place of the old party and old performance. A novation is not an assignment or delegation because neither party unilaterally introduces a third party into the contract. In a novation, all three parties agree. Because all parties agree, the old party can never be sued nor sue on the original contract.

Casualty to Identified Goods

As set forth above, when identified goods are destroyed, the duties under the contract are discharged.

Perfect Tender

Under the UCC, if there is a single delivery of goods, the duty to deliver must be undertaken perfectly. Nevertheless, if tender is not perfect, the Seller has the right to cure tender anytime up to the agreed upon time of performance.

Impracticability

Impracticability occurs when a party can't perform at the time because of some unforeseen, severe and unassumed event that makes it unreasonable to perform as written in the contract. If the event which makes performance impracticable is temporary, the duties are merely suspended until the event ceases, at which time the duties to perform arise promptly. If the event which makes performance impracticable is permanent, then it is likened to impossibility and there is a discharge of duties.

Frustration of Purpose

Frustration occurs when the purpose of the contract no longer exists. Therefore, if some unforeseen event acts to cancel the purpose of the contract, and both parties knew of the purpose of the contract, then all duties are discharged.

Breach of Contract and Remedies

A breach of contract occurs when one has an absolute duty to perform under a contract but fails to perform even though performance was not excused. The following remedies are available under the UCC for breach of contract.

Seller's Remedies

1. If during manufacture, Seller manufactures and Buyer breaches, Seller is entitled to do anything reasonable, e.g. continue to manufacture the goods and sell them as finished products;

2. If the Seller has shipped goods in transit to Buyer and Buyer breaches, Seller can stop the goods in transit. If the Buyer is insolvent, this rule applies to all goods so that they won't be delivered and fall into the hands of the

Buyer's creditors. However, if Buyer is merely breaching, then the Seller can only stop large shipments.

3. If the goods are already delivered, and the Buyer breaches, if the Buyer is insolvent, the Seller may reclaim the goods within 10 days after delivery. If the Buyer is not insolvent, the Seller must sue for breach of contract.

See UCC Section 2-703 at Appendix 1.

Seller's Right of Resale

1. The Seller has the right to find a substitute Buyer to buy the goods. To exercise that right, the Seller is required to give the Buyer notice of intention to resell the goods. That notice is excused if the goods are of the type that will perish or decline rapidly. The Seller must also make a commercially reasonable resale. If there is a resale, the Seller is entitled to recover the difference between the contract price and the resale price from the Buyer.

2. If there is no resale, the Seller can get a market price recovery standard of damages, which would be the difference between the contract price and the market price for the goods at the time and place of tender.

3. Sellers who sell goods for the same price all of the time and who, therefore, experience no change in market price, rendering the above two remedies ineffective, can sue the Buyer for the profit they would have made on the sale. This is referred to as *lost volume sales*.

4. Seller can sue the Buyer for the price of the goods whenever the goods are so unique that there is no resale value or market price. The Seller will then give the Buyer the goods. This is similar to specific performance in non-UCC contracts.

See UCC Section 2-706(1) at Appendix 1.

Buyer's Remedies

1. The Buyer can reject nonconforming goods anytime before the Buyer accepts the goods.

2. The Buyer can revoke acceptance of the goods if the Buyer thereafter realizes that there is a defect in the goods. However, the defect must be substantial because acceptance has already taken place. In addition, the defect must have been difficult to discover.

See UCC Section 2-711 at Appendix 1.

Buyer's Procedures to Exercise Remedies

1. The Buyer must give the Seller notice of the defect. Once the notice is given, the Buyer must wait for Seller's instructions. If Seller gives reasonable instructions, Buyer must follow them. However, if the Seller does not give any instructions, or gives unreasonable instructions, then the Buyer can do anything reasonable with the goods at the Seller's expense—e.g. sell the goods, return the goods, etc.

2. The Buyer must attempt to cover his losses, i.e., the Buyer must go out into the market place without unreasonable delay to buy a reasonable substitute for the goods. If the Buyer does that, he is entitled to receive the difference between the cost of covering the goods, and the contract price, so that the Buyer is made "whole."

3. To determine a market price recovery, the Buyer gets the difference between the market price when the Buyer learns of the breach and the contract price.

4. Whenever the subject matter of the contract is unique, the Buyer can sue the Seller to require that the goods be delivered.

CHAPTER 2:

UCC ARTICLE 2A - LEASES

In General

Prior to the addition of Article 2A to the Uniform Commercial Code, leases for goods were traditionally governed by UCC Articles 2 or 9, as well as common law personal property rules and principles related to real estate leases. However, this caused much confusion and resulted in a nonuniform application of the law to such leases.

In 1987, Article 2A was added to the UCC to regulate leases for goods. It was subsequently revised in 1990, and has already been adopted— or is being considered for adoption—in a number of states.

Scope of Coverage

Article 2A applies to any transaction, regardless of form, that creates a lease.

See UCC Section 2A-102 at Appendix 2.

A *lease* is defined as a transfer of the right to possession and use of *goods* for a *term* in return for *consideration*. Thus, a sale is not a lease. Goods are defined as all things which are movable at the time of identification to the lease contract. Goods do not include money, instruments, chattel paper or minerals prior to extraction.

Types of Leases

Consumer Lease

A consumer lease is one which is entered into between a *lessor*—i.e., one who is regularly engaged in the business of leasing or selling—and a *lessee*—i.e., a consumer who leases the goods primarily for personal, family or household use. In addition, there is a provision in the UCC for a monetary cap on the total amount of payments which may be made under the lease contract, excluding payments for options to renew or buy, to be considered a consumer lease.

Finance Lease

A finance lease involves three parties: the *lessor*, the *lessee*, and a *supplier*. Under a finance lease:

(i) the lessor does not select, manufacture or supply the goods being leased; and

(ii) the lessor acquires the goods or the right to possession and use of the goods in connection with the lease; and

(iii) one of the following occurs:

(A) the lessee must receive a copy of the contract under which the lessor acquired the goods, or the right to possession and use of the goods, before signing the lease contract; or

(B) the lessee's approval of the contract under which the lessor acquired the goods, or the right to possession and use of the goods, is a condition to the effectiveness of the lease contract; or

(C) the lessee, before signing the lease contract, receives an accurate and complete statement designating the promises and warranties, etc.; or

(D) if the lease is not a consumer lease, the lessor, before the lessee signs the lease contract, informs the lessee in writing: (a) of the supplier's identity, unless the lessee was responsible for selecting the supplier; (b) that the lessee is entitled to all promises and warranties provided to the lessor by the supplier; and (c) that the lessee may communicate directly with the supplier to receive an accurate and complete statement of the promises and warranties, etc.

An example of such an agreement would be a sale and lease back, where Lessee purchases goods from Supplier pursuant to a sales contract. Lessee then sells those same goods to Lessor, who simultaneously leases the goods back to Lessee pursuant to a lease contract. The original sales contract between Lessee and Supplier is then assigned to Lessor.

This satisfies the Article 2A requirements because (i) Lessor had nothing to do with the initial selection, manufacture or supply of the goods; (ii) Lessor bought the goods (from Lessee) at the same time he leased the goods to Lessee; and (iii) Lessor entered into the sales contract with Lessee at the same time he leased the equipment back to Lessee.

Unconscionability

If any lease term or clause is found by the court to be unconscionable—i.e., so one-sided and detrimental to the interest of one of the parties that it operates to render the contract unenforceable—the court may refuse to enforce the contract, or may enforce the contract without the unconscionable clause. The court will also take appropriate action if, in connection with a consumer lease, it is alleged that the lease was induced by unconscionable conduct.

In determining unconscionability, the court will generally give the parties a reasonable opportunity to present evidence concerning the alleged unconscionable term, clause or conduct.

See UCC Section 2A-108 at Appendix 2.

Statute of Frauds

In order to be legally enforceable, the payments under the lease contract, if there is no writing, must be less than $1,000, excluding payments for options to renew or buy.

A lease contract will be enforceable if there is a writing, signed by the party against whom enforcement is sought, or by his authorized agent. However, the writing must be sufficient to indicate that a lease contract has been made between the parties, and describe the goods leased and the term of the lease.

Nevertheless, if the lease contract does not satisfy the above requirements, it will still be enforceable if the goods are to be specially manufactured and are not suitable for lease or sale to others in the course of the lessor's business, and prior to the lessee's repudiation of the lease, the lessor began to manufacture the goods, or made commitments to obtain the goods.

In addition, if the lessee receives and accepts the goods, or makes an admission in court that the lease contract was made, it may be enforceable.

See UCC Section 2A-201 at Appendix 2.

Parol Evidence Rule

Under Article 2A, lease terms which are intended by the parties to be a final expression of their agreement may not be contradicted by evidence of any prior agreement, or of any contemporaneous oral agreement. This is known as the *Parol Evidence Rule*.

Nevertheless, such terms may be explained or supplemented by evidence of course of dealing, usage of trade, or course of performance. However, if the court finds that the writing is not intended as a complete and exclusive statement of the lease terms, the court may allow evidence of consistent additional terms.

See UCC Section 2A-202 at Appendix 2.

Formation

Under Article 2A, a lease contract may be made in any manner sufficient to show that an agreement was reached by the parties. This is so even if the exact time the agreement was reached is indefinite. Further, the contract will still be found valid even if one or more terms are missing, provided the parties intended to make the contract, and there is a reasonably certain basis for furnishing an appropriate remedy.

See UCC 2A-204 at Appendix 2.

Firm Offer

A *firm offer* by a merchant—i.e., a written offer which assures that the offer will be held open—is not revocable, even if there is a lack of consideration, during the time stated in the offer. A reasonable time period, not to exceed three months, will be inferred if no specific time period is stated in the offer. If the firm offer is stated on a form provided by the offeree, the offeror must also sign the form.

See UCC Section 2A-205 at Appendix 2.

Acceptance

An offer to make a lease contract must be construed as inviting acceptance in any manner and by any medium deemed reasonable under the circumstances, unless otherwise unambiguously indicated by the language or the circumstances. Further, where the beginning of the requested performance is a reasonable method of acceptance, an offeror who has not been notified of acceptance within a reasonable time may treat the offer as having lapsed before acceptance.

See UCC Section 2A-206 at Appendix 2.

Modification

Modifications to a lease contract need not be accompanied by consideration to be enforceable. However, if the lease contract does not permit modification or rescission unless it is in a signed writing, the modification would not be enforceable without such writing. Nevertheless, any form supplied by a merchant for this purpose must also be signed by the other party, unless the agreement is made between merchants.

See UCC Section 2A-208 at Appendix 2.

Warranties

Express Warranties

An express warranty by the lessor is created as follows:

1. Any affirmation of fact or promise concerning the goods creates an express warranty that the goods will conform to such representation.

2. Any description of the goods creates an express warranty that the goods will conform to such description.

3. Any sample or model of the goods creates an express warranty that the goods will conform to such sample.

In order to create an express warranty, it is not necessary that the lessor use any specific words, or that the lessor intended to create a warranty. However, a warranty is generally not created if the lessor merely states his opinion concerning the goods.

See UCC Section 2A-210 at Appendix 2.

Warranties Against Interference and Infringement

A lease contract contains a warranty that no person holds a claim to, or interest in, the goods during the lease term which will interfere with the lessee's enjoyment, resulting from any act or omission of the lessor.

Nevertheless, if a lessee furnishes specifications for the goods to the lessor or supplier, and they comply with the lessee's specifications for the goods, the lessor or supplier shall be held harmless—i.e., indemnified—by the lessee against any claim of infringement which arises out of such specifications.

See UCC Section 2A-211 at Appendix 2.

Implied Warranty of Merchantability

A warranty that goods will be merchantable is implied in a lease contract provided the lessor is a merchant with respect to goods of that kind. The minimum requirements for merchantability are set forth in the statute. This provision does not apply to finance leases.

See UCC Section 2A-212 at Appendix 2.

Implied Warranty of Fitness for a Particular Purpose

If at the time a lease contract is made, a lessor is told, or has reason to know, that the goods being leased are for a particular purpose, and the lessee is depending on the lessor's judgment to furnish suitable goods, an implied warranty that the goods will fit that purpose is implied in the contract. This provision does not apply to finance leases.

See UCC Section 2A-213 at Appendix 2.

Transfer of Rights Under Lease

In general, any interest of a party under a lease contract may be transferred, including rights under a sublease. However, if the lease contract prohibits transfers, or makes a transfer an event of default, the innocent party may seek to enforce the remedies available under Article 2A - Section 5 against the transferring party. Nevertheless, the transfer will still be deemed effective.

Effect of Lease Contract

A lease contract is generally effective and enforceable between the parties to the lease and third parties, provided the contract meets all other requirements for enforceability under Article 2A.

See UCC Section 2A-301 at Appendix 2.

CHAPTER 3:

UCC ARTICLE 3 - NEGOTIABLE INSTRUMENTS

In General

A negotiable instrument is generally defined as an unconditional promise or order to pay a fixed amount of money. To be considered "negotiable" an instrument must meet the requirements stated in UCC Article 3:

1. There must be a signed writing that orders or promises the payment of a fixed amount of money. For example, a draft must contain an "order" by the drawer, and a note must contain a "promise" by the maker.

2. The promise or order to pay money must be unconditional.

3. The amount of money to be paid must be "fixed" in the writing. For example, a draft must contain a sum certain, e.g. $500.00. A note must contain a set number of payments at a fixed sum, e.g. 12 monthly installments of $200 per month.

4. The instrument must be made "payable to bearer" or "payable to order." The significance of this clause is further discussed below.

5. The instrument must be payable on demand or at a definite time. If the instrument does not state any time for payment, it will be considered payable on demand.

Negotiable instruments do not include money; payment orders governed by UCC Article 4A; or investment securities governed by Article 8. Secured transactions may also contain negotiable instruments, however, they are primarily covered under UCC - Article 9. If there is a conflict between the UCC Articles, both Article 4 and 9 govern over Article 3.

Types of Negotiable Instruments

Drafts and notes are the two primary types of negotiable instruments:

Drafts

A draft involves three parties, and is also known as *three party paper*. The draft is issued by a *drawer*, and directed to a *drawee*, who is thereby *ordered* to unconditionally pay to the order of the *payee* the amount stated. A check is a type of draft.

The *drawer* is the person who signs the draft, or is otherwise identified in the draft as the person ordering payment to be made. The *drawee* is the person who is ordered by the drawer to make the payment. The *payee* is the person who is entitled to payment of the amount set forth in the draft, which is payable either on demand or at some definite time.

See UCC Section 3-108 at Appendix 3.

The drawer of the draft is liable to make good on the draft if it is dishonored by the drawee when presented for payment by the payee.

Notes

A note involves two parties, and is also known as *two party paper*. The note is issued by a *maker*, which unconditionally *promises* to pay to the order of the *payee*, a fixed amount of money, which is payable either on demand or at some definite time.

See UCC Section 3-108 at Appendix 3.

A distinction is drawn between a draft and a note in that a draft "orders" payment to be made, and a note "promises" that payment will be made.

A certificate of deposit is a type of note issued by a bank which acknowledges that a sum of money has been received by the bank, and promises to repay that money at some definite time. The payee generally has the option of taking the sum of money at that time, or of *rolling over* the money—i.e., keeping the money on deposit with the bank for another fixed period of time. Fees may be assessed by the bank if the payee withdraws funds from a certificate of deposit prior to its maturity date.

Uses of Negotiable Instruments

Checks and Drafts

A check is commonly used in business transactions to pay for goods, and serves as a substitute for cash payments. For example, a check may be safely sent through the mail between the parties whereas cash, unless sent by a registered and insured method, would be risky. In addition, a draft may be used by a Seller to collect money owed by the Buyer from the Buyer's Bank.

Notes

A note is generally used to defer payments on a purchase. For example: Buyer wishes to purchase a washing machine. However, due to limited funds, the Buyer would like to make monthly installment payments on the appliance. For that purpose, the Buyer may sign a *promissory note*, promising to make the monthly payments.

Indorsements

An *indorsement* is a signature which is made on an instrument by the *indorser*. An indorsement is made in order to (i) negotiate—i.e., transfer—the instrument; (ii) place a restriction on the payment of the instrument; or (iii) incur indorser's liability on the instrument. Words may accompany the indorsement.

The signature of a person as maker, drawer or acceptor of the instrument is not an indorsement. In addition, a signature would not be considered an indorsement if the accompanying words, terms of the instrument, or place of signature, etc., clearly indicate that the signature was made for a purpose other than indorsement.

Instrument Payable to Bearer or Order

If an instrument is payable "to the bearer," it can be negotiated merely by transferring possession of the instrument. If an instrument is payable "to the order of [an identified person]," it cannot be negotiated by transfer of possession without the indorsement of that person.

Instrument Payable to Bearer

An instrument is "payable to bearer" if:

1. The instrument states that it is "payable to bearer," or "payable to the order of bearer," or otherwise indicates that the person in possession is entitled to payment, and does not state an identified person as payee; or

2. The instrument states that it is "payable to cash," or "payable to the order of cash," or otherwise indicates that it is not payable to an identified person.

UCC Section 3-109 at Appendix 3.

An instrument "payable to bearer" may become payable to an identified person if it is *specially indorsed*. A special indorsement is one which identifies a person to whom the holder makes the instrument payable. Once specially indorsed, the instrument becomes payable to the identified person, and the instrument may be negotiated only by the indorsement of that person.

UCC Section 3-205(a) at Appendix 3.

Instrument Payable to Order

If the instrument is not "payable to the bearer," then it would be "payable to order." An instrument is "payable to order" if it names an identified person—e.g. "Payable to the order of [an identified person]." However, if the instrument is "payable to [an identified person] and bearer," it will be considered "payable to bearer."

UCC Section 3-109 at Appendix 3.

An instrument payable to an identified person may become payable to bearer if it is indorsed *in blank*. Unlike a special indorsement, a blank indorsement does not identify a specific person to whom the instrument is payable. Thus, the instrument then becomes payable to the bearer and may be negotiated by transfer of possession alone.

UCC Section 3-205(b) at Appendix 3.

The Holder in Due Course

The rule of derivative title, which is applicable in most areas of law, does not allow a property owner to transfer rights in a piece of property greater than his own. However, if an instrument is "negotiable," this rule is suspended. A good faith purchaser takes title to the instrument free of any defects or claims, and may acquire greater rights than the party who transferred those rights. This person is also known as a *holder in due course*.

Nevertheless, in order to have the rights of a holder in due course, the instrument must have appeared authentic when issued or negotiated to the holder, e.g. not forged or altered, and the holder must have paid value for the instrument in good faith without knowledge of any claims or defects in title, or that the instrument was dishonored.

For example: Seller contracts with Buyer for goods to be shipped. Buyer pays Seller for the goods by check. Seller indorses the check to Seller's Bank. In the meantime, Buyer receives the goods but rejects them due to defects. Buyer then stops payment on the check with his bank—the "drawee bank." When Seller's Bank presents the check to the drawee bank for payment, the check is dishonored. When Seller's Bank notifies Buyer that the check was dishonored, Buyer claims that the goods were defective, thus, there was no consideration given for the payment. Buyer claims lack of consideration as a defense against both the Seller and the Bank.

Real Defenses

Buyer's defense would be proper as it relates to his obligation to Seller. However, under Article 3, the Bank, as a *holder in due course*, is entitled to enforce its rights against the Buyer unless the Buyer has a "real" defense. Real defenses include (i) infancy; (ii) duress; (iii) lack of capacity; (iv) illegality of the transaction; (v) fraud; or (vi) discharge in bankruptcy. Thus, the defense of lack of consideration would not preclude the Bank from enforcing its rights against the Buyer.

See UCC Sections 3-302(a) and 3-305(a) at Appendix 3.

Additional Requirements

In order for the Bank to enforce its rights, the following conditions must also apply:

1. The instrument must be negotiable, as set forth above.

2. The taker of the instrument must be a holder—i.e., the person in possession—if the instrument is payable to bearer, or the identified person if such person is in possession.

3. The holder who takes the instrument must be a holder in due course, as set forth above.

Authorized Signatures

A person is not liable on an instrument unless that person signed the instrument, or the instrument was signed by an authorized representative—i.e., an agent. If the instrument is signed by an agent, the person who is being represented is bound to the same degree as if they signed the instrument personally, even if they are not identified in the instrument.

If an authorized representative signs his own name to the instrument, as the authorized representative of another, the representative is not personally liable on the instrument provided the form of the signature shows clearly that it is made on behalf of the represented person identified in the instrument.

However, if the form of the signature does not clearly show that it is being made in a representative capacity, and the represented person is not identified in the instrument, the representative is liable to any holder in due course that took the instrument without notice that the representative did not intend to be liable.

An unauthorized signature is ineffective except as the signature of the unauthorized signer, in favor of a person who, in good faith, pays the instrument or takes it for value.

See UCC Sections 3-401(a), 3-402 and 3-403(a).

Transfer Warranties

A person who transfers an instrument for consideration warrants to the transferee that (i) the warrantor is entitled to enforce the instrument; (ii) the signature is authentic and authorized; (iii) the instrument has not been altered; (iv) the instrument is not subject to a defense or claim in recoupment against the warrantor; and (v) the warrantor has no knowledge of any insolvency proceedings affecting the instrument.

If there occurs a breach of warranty, the transferee is entitled to recover damages from the warrantor in an amount equal to the loss suffered as a result of the breach, however, recovery is limited to the amount of the instrument plus expenses and loss of interest.

See UCC Section 3-416(a) and 3-426(b) at Appendix 3.

Discharge of Obligations

There are a number of ways in which the obligations under an instrument may be discharged, including but not limited to payment or cancellation of the instrument. Nevertheless, the discharge of a party's obligation to pay is not effective against a holder in due course without notice of the discharge.

Discharge by Payment

If payment is made by or on behalf of a party obligated to pay on an instrument, to a person entitled to enforce the instrument, the instrument is deemed paid and the party is discharged. This is so even if payment is made with the knowledge of a claim to the instrument by another person.

Nevertheless, a party's obligation to pay on an instrument is not discharged if a claim to the instrument is enforceable against the party receiving the payment, and (i) payment is made with the payor's knowledge that payment is prohibited pursuant to injunction or other court order; or (ii) except for a cashier check, teller check or certified check, the person holding the claim indemnifies the payor against loss resulting from the payor's refusal to pay the person entitled to enforce the instrument; or (iii) the payor knows the instrument is stolen and makes the payment to the person seeking payment knowing he is in wrongful possession of the instrument.

See UCC Sections 3-601 and 3-602 at Appendix 3.

Discharge by Cancellation

A person who is entitled to enforce an instrument may discharge the obligation of a party to pay on the instrument by (i) an intentional voluntary act, such as surrendering the instrument to that party, or destroying, mutilating or otherwise canceling the instrument; or (ii) by agreeing not to sue or otherwise giving up his rights in a signed writing.

See UCC Section 3-604(a) at Appendix 3.

CHAPTER 4:

UCC ARTICLE 4 - BANK DEPOSITS AND COLLECTIONS

In General

Banks and bank accounts are regulated by both state and federal statutory law. Title 12 of the Code of Federal Regulations contains federal agency regulations that concern banks and banking. Regulation J of the Federal Reserve comes into play if a check passes through the federal reserve system. Regulation CC extensively governs the availability of funds in a depositor's account and the process involving checks dishonored because of non-payment. Further, the timetable for making funds available for withdrawal after a check is deposited in a depositary bank is governed by the Expedited Funds Availability Act.

Banking activities are also governed by a number of UCC Articles. For example, checks and certificates of deposit are negotiable instruments under Article 3, as discussed in Chapter 3 of this almanac. In addition, Articles 4A, 5, and 8 deal with funds transfers, letters of credit, and securities, respectively.

This chapter is concerned with UCC Article 4, which sets forth the rights between parties with respect to bank deposits and collections. If there is a conflict among the Articles that deals with banking matters, Article 4 governs Article 3, but Article 8 governs Article 4.

Depositary and Collecting Banks

The first bank to take an item is called a *depositary bank*. The depositary bank may also be the *payor bank*, as discussed below. The other banks that subsequently handle the check, but are not responsible for its final payment. are called *collecting banks*.

Role of the Collecting Bank

While an item is in the process of collection, the collecting bank is an agent or sub-agent of the owner of the item—e.g., the payee who deposited the item—unless a contrary intent clearly appears. Any settlement given for the item is provisional until it becomes final. Because of the enormous volume of items which pass through collecting banks, it would be impossible to expect the bank to examine each indorsement, therefore, the fact of agency arises regardless of the form of indorsement on the item, or whether the item is indorsed at all. Nevertheless, any rights of the owner to the proceeds from the item are subject to the rights of the collecting bank.

See UCC Section 4-201(a) at Appendix 4.

The collecting bank is responsible for:

1. Presenting an item, or sending it for presentment.

2. Sending a notice of dishonor or nonpayment, or returning an item to the bank's transferor.

3. Settling for an item.

4. Notifying its transferor of any loss or delay in transit within a reasonable time after discovery.

In carrying out its functions, the collecting bank must exercise ordinary care. Ordinary care requires that the collecting bank take proper action following receipt of an item, notice, or settlement before its midnight deadline. The *midnight deadline* generally refers to midnight on the next banking day following the banking day on which the bank receives the item, notice, or settlement.

See UCC Section 4-202(a) and 4-202(b) at Appendix 4.

Role of the Depositary Bank

If a bank customer delivers an item to a depositary bank for collection, the depositary bank becomes a holder of the item provided the customer was the holder of the item, whether or not the customer actually indorses the item. If the bank satisfies all other requirements contained in UCC Section 3-302, the bank then becomes a *holder in due course*. The depositary bank warrants to the collecting banks, the payor bank and the drawer that the item was paid or deposited into the customer's account.

See UCC Section 4-205 at Appendix 4.

Transfer Warranties

A customer or collecting bank that transfers an item and receives settlement or other consideration warrants to the transferee and to any subsequent collecting bank that:

1. The warrantor is a person entitled to enforce the item;

2. All signatures on the item are authentic and authorized;

3. The item has not been altered;

4. The item is not subject to any third party claims that can be asserted against the warrantor; and

5. The warrantor is unaware of any insolvency proceedings concerning the maker.

If the item is dishonored, the warrantor is obligated to pay the amount due on the item. A warrantor cannot disclaim liability under this section. Thus, if a person takes the item in good faith, he may recover damages from the warrantor in an amount equal to the loss suffered as a result of the breach. However, recovery is limited to the amount of the instrument plus expenses and loss of interest.

See UCC Section 4-207 at Appendix 4.

Presentment Warranties

If an unaccepted draft is presented to the drawee bank for payment or acceptance, and the drawee pays or accepts the draft, the presenter and any prior transferor of the draft warrants to the drawee that:

1. The warrantor is, or was, a person entitled to enforce the draft;

2. The draft has not been altered;

3. The warrantor has no knowledge that the signature of the drawer is unauthorized.

If there is a breach of warranty, the drawee is entitled to damages in an amount equal to the amount paid by the drawee less the amount drawee received, or is entitled to receive, from the drawer, as well as expenses and loss of interest.

See UCC Section 4-208(a) at Appendix 4.

Payor Banks

The bank that is responsible for making payment on a check is called a *payor bank*. An item is deemed "finally paid" if:

1. The payor bank pays the item in cash to the presenter;

2. The payor bank settles for the item without having a right to revoke the settlement; or

3. The payor bank makes a provisional settlement for the item, and fails to revoke the settlement within the statutory time period.

If, however, the payor bank settles for a demand, other than a documentary draft or immediate payment over the counter, before midnight of the banking day of receipt, the payor bank is entitled to revoke and recover the settlement. However, before final payment and before the midnight deadline, the payor bank must:

1. Return the item; or

2. Send written notice of dishonor or nonpayment if the item is unavailable for return.

Charging the Customer's Account

A bank may charge a customer's account for an item that is properly payable from the account. An item is "properly payable" if the customer authorizes the item, and it is in accordance with any agreement between the customer and bank. As set forth below, the bank has a duty to the customer to make sure that it only makes payments on genuine orders of the customer.

Forged Checks

If the bank honors a check which bears a forged signature of the customer, the bank must credit the customer's account for the amount of the forged check.

Alterations

If the bank honors a check which the payee altered by increasing the amount payable, the bank must credit the customer's account with the amount of the altered check, less the original amount. For example, if the bank honors a check written for $50, which is altered to reflect a payable amount of $500, the bank must credit the customer's account for $450, the amount of the altered check less the original amount.

See UCC Section 4-401(d) at Appendix 4.

Postdated Checks

Due to the automated check collection process, if a bank charges a customer's account for a check that is postdated—i.e., presented for payment before its date—the bank may still charge the customer's account unless it receives notice from the customer describing the postdated check.

See UCC Section 4-401(c) at Appendix 4.

Overdraft

A bank may charge a customer's account even if the charge creates an overdraft to the account. However, a customer is not liable for the amount of the overdraft if he neither signed the item nor benefitted from its proceeds.

See UCC Section 4-401(a) and 4-401(b) at Appendix 4.

Old Checks

A bank is not obligated to pay a check which is presented more than six month after its date, unless the check is a certified check. Nevertheless, a bank may do so in good faith.

See UCC Section 4-404 at Appendix 4.

Stop Payment Order

A customer may order the bank to stop payment on any item, provided it gives the bank a description of the item in time for the bank to prevent taking action on the item. A stop-payment order is effective for six months and may be renewed. Nevertheless, if the stop payment order was verbal, and not confirmed, the stop payment order is only in effect for 14 days following the verbal order.

See UCC Section 4-403(a) and 4-403(b) at Appendix 4.

Documentary Drafts

A documentary draft is a check or other type of draft that will only be honored if certain papers are first presented to the payor of the draft. A bank presenting a documentary draft must deliver the documents to the drawee on acceptance of the draft provided it is payable more than three days after presentment. Otherwise, document delivery is required on payment.

If the draft is dishonored upon presentment for either payment or acceptance; the bank must notify the transferor; give the reasons for the dishonor, if known; and request further instructions. Alternatively, the bank may seek the services of a referee to resolve the matter.

See UCC Section 4-503 at Appendix 4.

CHAPTER 5:

UCC ARTICLE 4A - FUNDS TRANSFERS

In General

Funds transfers are governed by UCC Article 4A. A *funds transfer* is a series of transactions, beginning with the originator's payment order, made for the purpose of making payment to the beneficiary of the order. A funds transfer includes any payment order issued by the originator's bank, or an intermediary bank, which is intended to carry out the order. The funds transfer is completed when the beneficiary bank accepts the payment order for the benefit of the beneficiary. In most cases, the series of transactions is made electronically.

For example: Buyer and Seller enter into a contract for the sale of goods. Instead of sending Seller a check, Buyer wants to have his bank send the money to Seller's bank for credit to Seller's account. In order to accomplish this transfer of funds, Buyer must instruct his bank to carry out the transfer. Buyer's instruction is known as the *payment order*. Buyer is the *originator* of the payment order. Buyer's bank—the *originator's bank*—is known as the *receiving bank* because it "received" Buyer's payment order. Seller is the *beneficiary* of the payment order, and Seller's bank is known as the *beneficiary's bank*.

When Buyer's bank executes the payment order by instructing Seller's bank to credit Seller's account, Buyer's bank also becomes the "sender" of a payment order with respect to Seller's bank, and Seller's bank becomes the "receiving bank" with respect to that order. In cases where additional banks handle the transfer between the originator's bank and the beneficiary's bank, those banks are called *intermediary banks*.

Security Procedures

Problems in funds transfers may arise if there is an error in the payment order, or an unauthorized payment order. In order to prevent such problems, a security procedure may be established by agreement between the customer and the receiving bank—i.e., the originator's bank—which would require some security device to be used, e.g, the use of algorithms or other codes, identifying words or numbers, encryption, or callback procedures.

See UCC Section 4A-201 at Appendix 5.

Unauthorized Payment Orders

If the receiving bank carries out the agreed upon security procedure, the payment order will be deemed effective as to the customer's order whether or not it was authorized by the customer, provided that: (i) the security procedure is a commercially reasonable method of providing security against unauthorized payment orders; and (ii) the receiving bank proves that it accepted the payment order in good faith and in compliance with the security procedure.

Nevertheless, if the customer can prove that the unauthorized payment order: (i) was not directly or indirectly caused by a person who had authority to act on the customer's behalf; or (ii) was made by a person who obtained access to the customer's transmitting facility or who obtained information facilitating a breach of the security procedure from a source controlled by the customer, the receiving bank is not entitled to enforce or retain payment even if the customer is at fault.

See UCC Sections 4A-202(b) and 4A-203(2) at Appendix 5.

Erroneous Payment Orders

If an accepted payment order was transmitted pursuant to a security procedure which was supposed to detect errors, and the payment order erroneously: (i) instructed payment to an incorrect beneficiary; or (ii) instructed payment in an amount greater than authorized; or (iii) duplicated a previous payment order, the sender is not obligated to pay the order if he proves that he or his agent complied with the security procedure. If the funds transfer is completed, the bank is entitled to recover any amount paid to the beneficiary to the extent the funds were erroneously paid.

See UCC Section 4A-205 at Appendix 5.

Acceptance of Order

A receiving bank, not including a beneficiary's bank, is deemed to have accepted a payment order when it *executes* the order. Execution occurs when the receiving bank issues its own payment order, which is intended to carry out the payment order it originally received. A beneficiary's bank cannot execute a payment order, it can only accept it.

A beneficiary's bank is deemed to have *accepted* a payment upon the earliest happening of the following events:

1. The bank (i) pays the beneficiary; (ii) notifies the beneficiary that his account has been credited with the funds; or (iii) notifies the benefi-

ciary of receipt of the order provided the notice does not indicate that the order is being rejected or the funds being held until payment is received by the sender; or

2. The bank receives payment of the entire amount of the sender's payment order; or

3. The opening of the next "funds-transfer business day" following the payment date of the order, provided: (i) the amount of the order is fully covered by a credit balance in an authorized account of the sender; or (ii) the bank has received full payment from the sender, unless there has been a rejection of the order as set forth in the statute.

Nevertheless, acceptance of the order cannot occur: (i) before it is received by the receiving bank; or (ii) if the beneficiary does not have an account with the receiving bank.

See UCC Section 4A-209 at Appendix 5.

Misdescription of Beneficiary

Acceptance cannot occur where a payment order received by the beneficiary's bank identifies a nonexistent or unidentifiable person or account as beneficiary.

If the name and account number contained in the payment order identify two different persons, the beneficiary's bank may rely on the account number as the proper identification of the beneficiary if the bank is not aware of the conflict.

In that case, if the beneficiary's bank pays the person identified by account number, and the originator is a bank, the originator is obligated to pay the order. However, if the originator is not a bank, and proves that the beneficiary was not entitled to payment, the originator is not obligated to pay the order unless the originator's bank can prove that, prior to acceptance, the originator received notice that payment of the order might be made by the beneficiary's bank on the basis of the account number alone. In any event, the originator's bank may be able to recover any amount paid to a person who was not entitled to receive payment, as provided in the statute.

If the beneficiary's bank pays a person identified by name, or knows that the name and account number identify different persons, no person has rights as beneficiary except the person paid by the bank, provided that person was entitled to receive payment. However, if no identified person has rights as beneficiary, acceptance cannot occur.

See UCC Section 4A-207 at Appendix 5.

Rejection of Order

A payment order is deemed rejected when the receiving bank transmits a notice of rejection to the sender orally, electronically or in writing. A rejection notice does not require any specific words provided it clearly indicates that the order is being rejected. Rejection is effective when the notice is given if it is transmitted by reasonable means—e.g., by a means agreed to between the parties. If the means of transmission is deemed unreasonable—e.g., any means other than that agreed to unless no significant delay resulted from noncompliance—rejection is effective when the notice is received by the sender.

See UCC Section 4A-210(a) at Appendix 5.

Cancellation and Amendment of Order

The sender may transmit a communication to the receiving bank which cancels or amends the payment order orally, electronically, or in writing. The communication is effective if notice is received in time to give the receiving bank a reasonable opportunity to act prior to accepting the payment order.

If the receiving bank accepted the payment order prior to receiving the communication, cancellation or amendment is not effective (i) unless the receiving bank agrees; or (ii) unless otherwise authorized without agreement under a funds transfer system rule.

See UCC Section 4-211(a); 4-211(b) and 4-211(c) at Appendix 5.

Payment of Order

The day on which the amount of the payment order is made payable to the beneficiary by his bank is known as the "payment date." Although the payment date may be determined by the sender's instructions, it cannot occur before the order is received by the beneficiary's bank.

Once the beneficiary's bank accepts the order, the sender is obligated to pay the bank the amount of the order by the payment date. As it relates to a receiving bank other than the beneficiary's bank—e.g. an intermediary bank—the sender is obligated to pay the bank the amount of the order once the bank "accepts" the order, however, actual payment is not due until the bank "executes" the order—i.e., the receiving bank issues it own payment order intended to carry out the payment order it originally received.

Once the beneficiary's bank credits the beneficiary's account, payment to the beneficiary is deemed to have occured when: (i) the beneficiary is notified of the right of withdrawal; (ii) the credit is lawfully applied to a beneficiary's debt; or (iii) funds are otherwise made available to the beneficiary.

See UCC Sections 4A-401; 4A-402(a); 4A-402(b); 4A- 402(c) and 4A-405(a) at Appendix 5.

CHAPTER 6:

UCC ARTICLE 5 - LETTERS OF CREDIT

In General

The UCC defines a *letter of credit* as an engagement by a bank or other person, made at the request of the *customer*—e.g., the Buyer— that the *issuer* of the letter of credit—commonly the Buyer's bank—will honor drafts or other demands for payment by the *beneficiary*—e.g., the Seller—provided the conditions specified in the letter of credit are met.

A letter of credit is commonly used in contracts for the sale of goods. However, the issuance of a letter of credit is not limited to the sale of goods. For example, a letter of credit may also involve the sale or transfer of other items under the UCC, such as investment securities. For purposes of this chapter, a sales contract for goods between a Buyer and Seller will be used to illustrate the letter of credit transaction.

A Seller may want some guarantee of payment if the Seller ships goods to the Buyer pursuant to a sales contract. The letter of credit gives the Seller some assurance that he will not have to incur considerable expense in retrieving the goods if the Buyer reneges on the deal, thus minimizing his risks.

Procedure

If the Seller requires a letter of credit in order to complete a transaction, a specific provision is included in the contract between the Buyer and Seller which sets forth the conditions which must be met before the Buyer's bank will pay the Seller for the goods.

Although no particular form of phrasing is required, a letter of credit provision generally states that the Buyer will arrange for a letter of credit with the Buyer's Bank, to be issued in the purchase price amount, naming the Seller as the Beneficiary. To be valid, a letter of credit must be in writing and signed by the Issuer. If the Buyer fails to furnish the letter of credit within the required time, this constitutes a breach of the sales contract.

See UCC Section 5-104(a) at Appendix 6.

The letter of credit provision will also specify the required documentation the Seller needs to present to the Buyer's bank in order to receive payment for the goods. For example, the bank may require, among other things, an invoice, an inspection certificate, and/or an insurance policy covering the goods. In addition, the provision may require that the Seller comply with the conditions by a certain date. When the Seller presents his demand for payment to the issuing bank, he is warranting—i.e., making a representation—that he has complied with all of the terms set forth in the letter of credit.

See UCC Section 5-111(1) at Appendix 6.

In order to provide the Seller with a letter of credit, the Buyer enters into an agreement with the issuing bank, under which the Buyer agrees to pay the bank a service fee, and to reimburse the bank for payment made to the Seller under the letter of credit. Such reimbursement is made after the bank honors the request for payment by the Seller. The bank then surrenders the bill of lading to the Buyer, who presents the bill to the Carrier to obtain the goods.

If the bank is lending the Buyer the money to purchase the goods, the bank retains a purchase money security interest in the bill of lading and the goods.

Establishment of the Letter of Credit

The letter of credit is deemed "established" as follows:

As to the Buyer, it is established as soon as either (i) the letter of credit is sent to the Buyer; or (ii) an authorized written advice of the issuance of the credit is sent to the Seller. Once an irrevocable credit is established as to the Buyer, it cannot be modified or revoked without the consent of the Buyer.

As to the Seller, it is established when he receives the letter of credit or an authorized written advice of its issuance. Once an irrevocable credit is established as to the Seller, it cannot be modified or revoked without the consent of the Seller.

See UCC Section 5-106(1) and 5-106(2) at Appendix 6.

Advising Bank

Once the letter of credit is issued, it is forwarded to the *advising bank*, which informs the Seller that the Buyer's bank has issued the credit. The advising bank is limited to this task, and does not play any role in honoring the letter of credit or issuing any payments under the credit.

See UCC Section 5-107(1) at Appendix 6.

Confirming Bank

If, as an extra measure of protection, the Seller engages a *confirming bank*, that bank would become directly obligated to the Seller for payments under the credit as if it were the issuing bank. A confirmation must be in writing and signed by the confirming bank to be valid. In addition, any modification of the terms of the credit must also be signed by the confirming bank, if one is engaged.

See UCC Section 5-107(2) at Appendix 6.

Liability of Issuing Bank

The issuing bank's responsibility is to make sure that the Seller has complied with all of the terms set forth in the letter of credit, e.g. presentation of required documentation. However, it is not the issuing bank's responsibility to make sure that the goods conform to the underlying contract between the Buyer and Seller, and it is not liable therefor.

If the Seller, or Seller's bank, presents the documentation required by the terms of the letter of credit, the bank will honor the demand for payment. If the bank does not honor the demand, it will be liable to the Seller. In that event, the Seller may recover the face amount of the demand, together with incidental damages and interest, less any amount obtained by resale or other use of the goods.

If, however, the bank honors the request for payment, and it is determined that the documentation did not comply with the letter of credit terms, the issuing bank will be liable to the Buyer.

See UCC Section 5-114(1) and 5-115 at Appendix 6.

Nevertheless, the Buyer may obtain assurances that the goods conform to the contract in other ways. For example, one of the conditions in the letter of credit may be the issuance of an inspection certificate by a designated third party. In addition, if an insurance policy covering the goods is a condition, the Buyer's interests will also be protected.

CHAPTER 7:

UCC ARTICLE 6 - BULK SALES

In General

UCC Article 6 was formerly entitled "Bulk Transfers." It addressed situations where an indebted merchant would sell his entire inventory to another for a price, keep the proceeds and fail to pay his creditors. In an attempt to protect defrauded creditors, former Article 6 required the merchant to give advance notice to his creditors that he was selling his inventory.

Advance notice required: (i) a list of the merchant's creditors; (ii) a schedule of the property to be sold; and (iii) notice to the creditors providing information about the sale. Notice was required to be given at least 10 days prior to the earlier of the transferee: (i) taking possession, or (ii) making payment. This advance notice gave the creditors a chance to impound the proceeds from the sale if necessary to protect their interests.

If the merchant failed to give advance notice and sold his inventory, the sale was ineffective as it related to the creditors, and the creditors could disregard the transfer and levy the goods as if they were never sold to the transferee.

In 1989, Article 6 was revised and renamed "Bulk Sales." States were given the option of selecting two alternatives: (i) Alternative A, which repealed Article 6; or (ii) Alternative B, which revised Article 6. This chapter discusses Alternative B—Revised Article 6.

Applicability

The provisions of UCC Article 6 apply to a bulk sale if:

1. The Seller's principal business is the sale of inventory from stock; and

2. The Seller is located in the particular state, or if located outside the United States, the Seller maintains a major executive office in the United States in the particular state.

In addition, the value of the property available to creditors must be in excess of $10,000, but can be no more than $25,000.

See UCC Section 6-103(1) and 6-103(3)(l) at Appendix 7.

Buyer's Obligations

In connection with a bulk sale transaction, the Buyer is required to:

1. Obtain from the Seller a list of all of Seller's business names and addresses for the past three years;

2. Unless excused by statute, obtain from the Seller a verified dated list of known claimants, including their names, addresses, and the amount of each claim;

3. Prepare or obtain from the Seller a schedule of distribution;

4. Give the required notice of the bulk sale as set forth in the statute;

5. Unless excused by statute, distribute the net contract price in accordance with the schedule of distribution;

6. Unless excused by statute, make the list of claimants available by (i) delivering a list to any claimant, upon written request, without charge; (ii) permitting any claimant to inspect and copy the list; or (iii) filing the list in the appropriate governmental office.

See UCC Section 6-104 at Appendix 7.

Notice to Claimants

In order to fulfill the notice obligation, the Buyer is required to deliver a written notice of the bulk sale to each claimant on the list, and to any other known claimant. Nevertheless, if the number of claimants exceeds two hundred, the Buyer may comply with the notice obligation by filing a written notice of the bulk sale in the appropriate governmental office, e.g. The Secretary of State.

A copy of the schedule of distribution must accompany the written notice of bulk sale, and the notice must provide the information required under the statute. Notice is required to be given not less than 45 days before the bulk sale takes place.

Liability of Buyer for Noncompliance

If a Buyer does not comply with the statutory requirements concerning creditors, the sale is still valid, however, the Buyer may be liable for damages caused by noncompliance. Damages are generally limited to the amount of the creditor's claim reduced by any amount the creditor would not have realized if the Buyer had complied.

In any action for noncompliance, the creditor has the burden of establishing the validity and amount of their claim, and the Buyer has the burden of establishing the amount that the creditor would not have realized if the Buyer had complied with the statutory requirements.

See UCC Section 6-107(1) and 6-107(2) at Appendix 7.

CHAPTER 8:

UCC ARTICLE 7 - WAREHOUSE RECEIPTS, BILLS OF LADING AND OTHER DOCUMENTS OF TITLE

In General

A *document of title* under the UCC includes a bill of lading, dock warrant, dock receipt, warehouse receipt, order for the delivery of goods, and any other document which in the regular course of business or financing is treated as adequate evidence that the person in possession of the document is entitled to receive, hold and dispose of the document and the goods it covers.

A document of title is deemed negotiable if its terms indicate that the goods are to be delivered "to bearer" or "to the order of a named person." Any other document is deemed non-negotiable. This chapter discusses two common documents of title: the warehouse receipt and the bill of lading.

Warehouse Receipts

A receipt issued by a person engaged in the business of storing goods for hire is called a *warehouse receipt.* The person who engages in the business of storing goods for hire is called a *warehouseman.* The person who enters into the agreement to have goods stored in the warehouse is known as a *bailor* and the warehouseman who takes possession of the goods is known as the *bailee.*

A warehouse receipt must contain the following information: (i) the location of the warehouse where the goods are stored; (ii) the date the receipt was issued; (iii) the consecutive number assigned to the receipt; (iv) a statement indicating whether the goods will be delivered to the bearer, or to a specified person; (v) the storage and handling charges; (vi) a description of the goods and their packaging; (vii) the signature of the warehouseman or his agent; and (viii) a statement indicating whether the warehouseman owns the goods solely or jointly. If so, the fact of such ownership must be indicated along with the amount of any liens or security interests claimed by the warehouseman.

Bill of Lading

A *bill of lading* is defined as a document evidencing the receipt of goods for shipment issued by a person engaged in the business of transporting or forwarding goods. The person named in the bill to whom the bill promises delivery is known as the *consignee*, and the person from whom the goods have been received for shipment is known as the *consignor*.

See UCC Sections 7-201(1); 7-202(1); and 7-202(2) at Appendix 8.

Liability

Liability of Warehouseman

A warehouseman is liable for damages for loss of, or injury to, stored goods which is caused by his failure to exercise such care as a reasonably careful person would exercise under like circumstances. However, unless otherwise agreed to, the warehouseman is not liable for any damages which were unavoidable even by exercise of the duty of care.

Nevertheless, there may be a limitation on liability clause in the warehouse receipt or storage agreement, which sets forth a specific liability amount per item. In that case, the warehouseman would not be liable for any damages which exceed this amount. However, it the warehouseman converts stored goods to his own use, any such limitation on liability is ineffective.

See UCC Sections 7-204(1) and 7-204(2) at Appendix 8.

Liability of Carrier

A carrier who issues a bill of lading must exercise the degree of care in relation to the goods which a reasonably careful person would exercise under like circumstances. Damages may be limited by a provision in the document. However, it the carrier converts the goods to his own use, any such limitation on liability is ineffective.

See UCC Section 7-309(1) and 7-309(2) at Appendix 8.

Warehouseman's Right to Terminate Storage

Upon expiration of the storage agreement—or if no expiration date is fixed, within a stated period of time not less than 30 days from the notice—a warehouseman may notify the bailor, or anyone having a claim to the goods, that the goods must be removed. If the goods are not removed by the date specified, the warehouseman is entitled to sell the goods according to a warehouseman's lien as set forth below.

See UCC Section 7-206(1) at Appendix 8.

Liens

Warehouseman's Lien

A warehouseman has a lien against the bailor on any goods covered by the warehouse receipt, or on the proceeds from the sale of the goods, for costs incurred, including storage, transportation, insurance, labor, and any other necessary expenses related to the goods. Nevertheless, a warehouseman loses his lien on any goods which he voluntarily delivers, or unjustifiably refuses to deliver.

A warehouseman's lien may be enforced by public or private sale of the goods, after notifying all persons who are known to claim any interest in the goods to be sold. The notice must contain a statement of the amount due, and the nature, time, and place of the sale.

See UCC Section 7-209(1); 7-209(4) and 7-210(1) at Appendix 8.

Carrier's Lien

A carrier has a lien on goods covered by a bill of lading for charges incurred subsequent to the date the goods were received for storage or transportation, and for any necessary expenses related to the preservation of the goods in connection with their transportation, or reasonably incurred in selling the goods pursuant to law.

The carrier's lien is effective against the consignor of the goods, unless the carrier had notice that the consignor lacked authority to subject the goods to such charges. Nevertheless, a carrier loses his lien on any goods which he voluntarily delivers or unjustifiably refuses to deliver.

A carrier's lien may be enforced by public or private sale of the goods, after notifying all persons who are known to claim any interest in the goods to be sold. The notice must contain a statement of the amount due, and the nature, time, and place of the sale.

See UCC Section 7-307(1); 7-307(2); and 7-308(1) at Appendix 8.

Obligation to Deliver

The bailee—e.g. the warehouseman or consignee—must deliver the goods to the person entitled to the goods pursuant to the document of title. Under the UCC, the "person entitled under the document" refers to the holder in the case of a negotiable document, or the person to whom delivery is to be made by the terms of written instructions under a non- negotiable document. Nevertheless, the person claiming the goods must satisfy the bailee's lien.

If the bailee delivers or otherwise disposes of goods in good faith, according to the terms of the document of title, he is not liable even though (i) the person from whom he received the goods had no authority to procure the document or dispose of the goods; and (ii) the person to whom he delivered the goods had no authority to receive them.

See UCC Section 7-404 at Appendix 8.

Negotiation of Document

A negotiable document of title "to the order of a named person" is negotiated by that person's indorsement and delivery. If the indorsement is made "in blank" or "to bearer," any person can negotiate by delivery alone. However, if it has been indorsed to a specified person, indorsement by the special indorsee as well as delivery is required for negotiation. A negotiable document of title, which by its original terms are "to bearer" may be negotiated by delivery alone.

A further discussion of negotiable instruments is set forth in Chapter 3.

Warranties

When a person negotiates or transfers a document of title for value, unless otherwise agreed, he warrants to his immediate purchaser that (i) the document is genuine; (ii) he has no knowledge of any fact which would impair its validity or worth; and (iii) his negotiation or transfer is rightful and fully effective with respect to the document of title and the goods it covers.

See UCC Section 7-507 at Appendix 8.

Missing Documents of Title

If a document of title is lost, stolen or destroyed, a court may order delivery of the goods, or issuance of a substitute document, and the bailee may comply with such court order without liability to any person.

If a bailee delivers goods to a person without such court order, he is liable to any person injured thereby, and if the delivery is not in good faith, the bailee becomes liable for conversion.

See UCC Section 7-601 at Appendix 8.

CHAPTER 9:

UCC ARTICLE 8 - INVESTMENT SECURITIES

In General

This chapter deals with the transfer of investment securities under UCC Article 8. Although this transaction is not a "sale of goods" under Article 2, the drafters believed that some aspects closely paralleled such transactions, meriting its inclusion in the UCC.

An investment security is an instrument: (i) issued in *bearer* or *registered* form as a type commonly recognized as a medium for investment; and (ii) evidencing a share or other interest in the property or enterprise of the issuer.

A security is either *certificated* or *uncertificated*. A certificated security is a negotiable instrument, whereas an uncertificated security is not represented by an instrument.

Issuer of Securities

The issuer of a security is one who:

1. Places or authorizes the placement of his name on a certificated security to: (i) evidence that the instrument represents a share, participation or other interest in his property or an enterprise; or (ii) evidence his duty to perform an obligation represented by the instrument;

2. Creates shares, participations or other interests in his property or in an enterprise, or undertakes obligations, relating to uncertificated securities;

3. Directly or indirectly creates fractional interests in his rights or property which are represented by certificated securities; or

4. Becomes responsible for, or in place of, any other person described as an issuer.

Transfer of Securities

Statute of Frauds

As with the sale of goods under Article 2, in order to be enforceable, a contract for the sale of securities must comply with the statute of frauds. Under Article 8, compliance with the statute of frauds is satisfied if there is:

1. A writing signed by the party against whom enforcement is sought, which is sufficient to indicate that a contract has been made for the sale of a stated quantity of described securities at a defined price; or

2. Delivery and acceptance of a certificated security or transfer instruction; or

3. Registration of the transfer of an uncertificated security where the transferee has failed to send written objection to the issuer within 10 days following receipt of the initial transaction statement confirming the registration; or

4. Payment; or

5. A writing sent within a reasonable time to the party against whom enforcement is sought, which confirms the sale or purchase, provided that party fails to send written objection within 10 days after its receipt; or

6. An admission—e.g., in pleadings or testimony—by the party against whom enforcement is sought, that a contract was made for the sale of a stated quantity of described securities at a defined price.

See UCC Section 8-319 at Appendix 9.

Certificated Security

The transfer of a certificated security occurs (i) at the time the purchaser takes possession of the certificated security; (ii) when a financial intermediary acquires possession issued or specially indorsed in the name of the purchaser; (iii) when a financial intermediary sends the purchaser confirmation of the purchase; or (iv) when a third person, not a financial intermediary, acknowledges that he is in possession of an identified certificated security and that he is holding it for the purchaser.

A *financial intermediary* refers to a bank, broker, clearing corporation or other person which, in the ordinary course of its business maintains security accounts for its customers and is acting in that capacity. In addition, the financial intermediary may have a security interest in securities that are held in the account for its customer.

See UCC Sections 8-313(1)(a); 8-313(1)(c); 8-313(1)(d) and 8-313(1)(e) at Appendix 10.

Uncertificated Security

The transfer of an uncertificated security occurs (i) at the time the transfer, pledge or release of the uncertificated security is registered to the purchaser or his agent; or (ii) when a pledge or transfer of the uncertificated security is registered by a third party and the third party acknowledges that he is holding it for the purchaser.

See UCC Section 8-313(1)(b) and 8-313(1)(f) at Appendix 9.

Purchaser's Right to Proof of Transferor's Authority

A purchaser of securities is entitled, on demand, to proof of the authority of the transferor to: (i) transfer, pledge, or release the security; or (ii) obtain registration of a transfer, pledge or release of a security. Nevertheless, if the purchase is not for value, the purchaser may be required to pay any necessary related expenses.

See UCC Section 8-316 at Appendix 9.

Duty to Transfer

The following rules apply to the sale of a security which is made on an exchange or otherwise transacted through brokers:

Selling Customer

The selling customer's duty to transfer is fulfilled when he: (i) places a certificated security in the possession of the selling broker; (ii) causes an uncertificated security to be registered in the name of the selling broker; (iii) causes an acknowledgment to be made to the selling broker that a certificated or uncertificated security is being held for him; or (iv) places a transfer instruction for an uncertificated security in the possession of the selling broker.

Selling Broker

The selling broker's duty to transfer is fulfilled when he: (i) places a certificated security in the possession of the buying broker; (ii) causes an uncertificated security to be registered in the name of the buying broker; (iii) places a transfer instruction for an uncertificated security in the possession of the buying broker; or (iv) effects clearance of the sale in accordance with the rules of the exchange on which the transaction took place.

Transferor

A transferor's duty to transfer a security under a contract of purchase is not fulfilled until he: (i) places a certificated security in the purchaser's possession in a form to be negotiated by purchaser; (ii) causes an uncertificated security to be registered in the purchaser's name; or (iii) at the purchaser's request, causes an acknowledgement to be made to the purchaser that a certificated or uncertificated security is being held for purchaser.

Wrongful Transfers

If a security is wrongfully transferred—e.g. because the owner was incapacitated—the owner may (i) reclaim possession of the certificated security; (ii) obtain possession of a new certificated security representing the same rights; (iii) compel an instruction to transfer an uncertificated security to owner representing the same rights; or (iv) sue for damages.

See UCC Section 8-315 at Appendix 9.

CHAPTER 10:

UCC ARTICLE 9 - SECURED TRANSACTIONS

In General

A debt is generally defined as an obligation or liability to pay. Debts may be "secured" or "unsecured." Unsecured debts—the most common type of consumer debt—are those for which the lender has retained no interest in any of the items purchased. Thus, if the debtor defaults on the payments, the lender has no legal right to repossess any of the goods. Examples of unsecured debts are credit card debt, medical expenses and uncollateralized loans.

A transaction is "secured" if the lender, by agreement, has retained some kind of interest in the borrower's property in return for making the loan. Secured debts usually involve large purchases, such as homes, automobiles, appliances and furniture. This security gives the lender some assurance that the debt will be repaid, or that the lender will not suffer a total loss if the borrower defaults. The secured item can be repossessed.

For example, when a home is purchased, the bank or mortgage company which finances the purchase retains the right to foreclose and sell the house if the payments are not made as agreed. The house is the security for the loan.

If an individual borrows money from a lending institution, such as a bank or finance company, the lender may require the borrower to pledge some item of value as *collateral* for the loan, such as a car. The loan is secured by the collateral, even though the collateral has nothing to do with the reason for borrowing the money.

A security interest also provides the secured party with the assurance that if the debtor files bankruptcy, the lender may be able to recover the value of the loan by taking possession of the collateral, instead of receiving only a fraction of the borrower's property after it is divided among all creditors, or nothing at all.

UCC Article 9 governs *secured* transactions. Because a security agreement is also a contract, it must comply with any other state laws governing contracts. Thus, the reader is advised to further check the law of his or her own jurisdiction when researching a specific issue.

Scope and Purpose

Article 9 applies to any transaction which is intended to create a security interest in personal property or fixtures, including goods, documents, instruments, general intangibles, chattel paper or accounts; and to sales of chattel paper or accounts. Article 9 also applies to security interests created by contract, as set forth in the statute. The purpose of Article 9 is to include all *consensual* security interests in personal property and fixtures under one Article.

See UCC Sections 9-102(1) and 9-102(2) at Appendix 10.

Exclusions

Exclusions from Article 9 include but are not limited to landlord's liens, transfers of employee wage claims; governmental transfers; transfers of insurance claims; transfers of real estate liens or leases; and transfers of tort claims. In addition, statutory liens are not governed by Article 9, but by the individual statute that creates them. Statutory liens may take priority over a perfected security interest unless the statute provides otherwise.

See UCC Sections 9-102(2); 9-104 and 9-310 at Appendix 10.

Attachment of a Security Interest

Statute of Frauds

Unless the secured party is in possession of the collateral pursuant to agreement—i.e., the collateral is "pledged"—a security interest is not enforceable against the debtor or third parties, and cannot attach until the debtor has signed a security agreement. The agreement to provide for a security interest must be in writing, signed by the debtor, and must describe the collateral.

The requirement of a writing is for evidentiary purposes in case a future conflict arises over the terms of the agreement and the identity of the collateral. Therefore, if the collateral is pledged, the need for a writing is of less importance and thus not required by the statute. Additional terms in a security agreement may include the amount of the debt and terms of repayment; and risk of loss and insurance provisions.

Value

Value must be given in return for the security interest in order for it to attach. Value refers to any consideration sufficient to support a simple contract. For example: Buyer purchases a washing machine from Seller on an installment basis. Buyer and Seller agree that Seller will retain a security interest in the washing machine in case Buyer reneges on the payments. The sale of the washing machine to Buyer is the consideration which supports the contract.

Debtor's Rights in Collateral

A security interest cannot attach until the debtor has rights in the collateral.

Pledged Security Agreement

A pledged security agreement exists when the debtor transfers the collateral to the secured party in exchange for a loan. An example of a pledged security agreement would be where an individual leaves an item with a pawnbroker in return for a cash payment and the right to redeem the item.

See UCC Section 9-203(1) at Appendix 10.

Perfection

The "perfection" of a security agreement allows a secured party to gain priority to the collateral over any third party. In general, the secured party is protected against any subsequent creditors and transferees of the debtor. In addition, the secured party's interest is superior to those of unsecured creditors in bankruptcy proceedings instituted by or against the debtor.

To perfect a security agreement, the filing of a financing statement is generally required unless an exception exists, as set forth in the statute. The purpose of the filing is to give public notice of the security interest. In general, most financing statements, other than those regarding land-related collateral, must be filed with the register of deeds in the county of the debtor's residence.

The financing statement generally must contain:

1. The names and addresses of the debtor and the secured party;

2. A description of the collateral; and

3. The signature of the debtor.

However, if the security agreement itself contains the above information, its filing may be sufficient to comply with this section.

See UCC Section 9-402(1) and 9-402(2) at Appendix 10.

Again, an exception to the filing requirement exists if the secured party takes possession of the security interest. If filing or possession takes place prior to attachment, the security interest is perfected at the time the requirements of attachment are met as set forth above

Assignment of Perfected Security Interest

If the secured party assigns a perfected security interest to another, the perfected status of the security interest against creditors of the original debtor remains intact, and no further filing is required.

See UCC Sections 9-302; 9-304 and 9-305 at Appendix 10.

Collateral

Article 9 defines *collateral* as property subject to a security interest, including accounts and chattel paper. Chattel paper refers to a writing which evidences both a monetary obligation and a security interest in goods. The collateral may remain in the possession of the debtor, or may be placed in the possession of the secured party, while the debt remains unpaid.

Rights and Duties of Secured Party in Possession of Collateral

If the secured party is in possession of the collateral, he is required to use reasonable care in preserving the collateral. However, the obligation to pay reasonable expenses is chargeable to the debtor, and also secured by the collateral. A type of such expense is insurance coverage. Thus, the risk of accidental loss or damage to the collateral is borne by the debtor if there is insufficient insurance coverage.

The secured party is entitled to hold any increase or profits received from the collateral as additional security, other than money. If the collateral generates any money, the secured party must turn it over to the debtor, or apply it to reduce the secured obligation. Collateral may be repledged by the secured party provided it does not impair the debtor's right to redeem the collateral.

If the secured party fails to meet the obligations imposed under the statute, he is liable for any resulting loss. However, the secured party does not thereby lose his security interest.

See UCC Section 9-207 at Appendix 10.

Collateral Owned by Non-Debtor

If the secured party is aware that collateral is owned by a non-debtor, the owner is not liable for the debt. In addition, the owner has the same right as the debtor to: (i) receive a statement of account; (ii) receive notice of and make objections to a secured party's proposal to retain the collateral to satisfy the debt; (iii) redeem the collateral; (iv) obtain injunctive relief; and (v) recover losses caused by the secured party's actions or inactions.

See UCC Section 9-112 at Appendix 10.

Release of Collateral

A secured party may release all or a part of any collateral described in a filed financing statement by signing a statement of release. The statement of release must contain: (i) a description of the collateral being released; (ii) the names and addresses of the debtor and secured party; and (iii) the financing statement file number.

See UCC Section 9-406 at Appendix 10.

Default

Whether a debtor is in default depends on the terms of the security agreement. For example, an agreement will invariably provide that failure to make payments required under the agreement constitutes default.

Rights and Remedies of Secured Party after Default

In addition to any rights and remedies provided in the security agreement in case of default, Article 9 affords the secured party further relief. For example, the secured party may execute against—i.e., reduce the claim to judgment and request the sheriff to levy—the debtor's property, which is then sold and the proceeds applied to the debt. If the agreement covers both real and personal property, he may foreclose on the real property.

In addition, the secured party may take possession of the collateral, if it is not already in his possession, or may sell the collateral and apply the proceeds of the sale to satisfy the claim. Of course, if there is any deficiency after sale—an amount still owing after the sale proceeds have been applied to the debt—the debtor is still liable for the deficiency, unless the underlying transaction is a sale of accounts or chattel paper and the security agreement provides for a deficiency judgment.

See UCC Sections 9-501 at Appendix 10.

Rights and Remedies of Debtor after Default

Right to Redemption

At any time before the secured party has disposed of the collateral, the debtor—or another secured party—may redeem the collateral by fulfilling the obligations secured by the collateral, as well as reimbursing the secured party for any expenses reasonably incurred in connection with the debtor's default. This may include legal fees and costs.

Written Notice of Secured Party's Intention to Retain Collateral

If a secured party proposes to retain the collateral in full satisfaction of the obligation, written notice of the proposal must be sent to the debtor absent the debtor's prior renunciation of the collateral. If the debtor fails to object, the secured party may retain the collateral.

Right to Reasonable Notification of Sale

Unless the collateral is perishable or subject to a rapid decline in value, the debtor is entitled to reasonable notice of the time and place of any public sale, or of the time after which any private sale is to be made.

Right to Accounting

If the security agreement secures an indebtedness, the secured party must account to the debtor for any surplus proceeds resulting from a sale of the collateral. However, if the underlying transaction is a sale of accounts or chattel paper, the debtor is only entitled to an accounting and surplus if the agreement provides for it.

CHAPTER 11:

PROPOSED UCC ARTICLE 2B - LICENSING

In General

The National Conference of Commissioners on Uniform State Laws (NCCUSL) and the American Law Institute (ALI) are presently in the last stages of finalizing UCC Article 2B - Licensing. Article 2B concerns transactions that largely have never been covered by the UCC.

The industries and transactions affected by Article 2B involve subject matter unlike the traditional UCC focus on goods. In Article 2B transactions, the value lies in intangibles: information and rights to use information. Article 2B will govern transactions involving software, on-line and internet services, cable television service, and licenses involving data, text, images and similar information, including contracts to write books, or to show films. In addition, if Article 2B is adopted by the states, it will be the dominant source of law governing software quality.

Critics of the proposed Article argue that it threatens to eliminate long-established customer protections and drastically extends the intellectual property rights of software publishers beyond what they are entitled to under Copyright law.

Scope of Article 2B

Section 2B-103 of the Article 2B Draft sets forth the proposed scope of the statute:

SECTION 2B-103. SCOPE.

(a) Except as otherwise provided in Section 2B-104 on excluded transactions and in subsection (b), this article applies to:

(1) any transaction that creates a software contract, access contract, or license; and

(2) any agreement to provide support for, maintain, or modify information related to a contract within the scope of this article.

(b) If this article governs part of a transaction and other contract law governs part, the following rules apply:

(1) This article applies to the information, informational rights, copies that contain the information, its packaging, and its documentation.

(2) Article 2 or 2A governs as to goods not within paragraph (1) and as to subject matter that is excluded under Section 2B-104(3).

(3) The rules of this article on contract formation apply to the entire transaction if:

(A) the parties agree to be bound by those rules; or

(B) except with respect to subject matter of paragraph (2), the transaction involves services or other subject matter not within this article or Article 2 or Article 2A and the information or services that are within the scope of this article are the predominant purpose of the transaction.

(c) The parties may agree that this article governs in whole or in part any transaction or a part thereof not otherwise within the scope of this article. Such an agreement is not effective to the extent it:

(1) would alter mandatory consumer protection rules that apply under otherwise applicable law; or

(2) applies to a transaction to which this article does not otherwise apply and that is governed by Article 2 or Article 2A.

Section 2B-104 of the Article 2B Draft sets forth the transactions that are proposed to be excluded from the statute.

SECTION 2B-104. TRANSACTIONS EXCLUDED FROM ARTICLE.

This article does not apply to the extent that a transaction:

(1) is a license or software contract that as between the licensor and licensee is only an incident of subject matter not governed by this article;

(2) is a license of a trademark, trade name, trade dress, patent, or related know-how not associated with a license or software contract that is otherwise covered by this article;

(3) is a sale or lease of a copy of a computer program as part of a sale or lease of goods that contain the computer program unless:

(A) the goods are merely a copy of the program;

(B) the goods are a computer or computer peripheral; or

(C) giving the purchaser of the goods access to or use of the computer program is a material purpose of the transaction;

(4) provides access to, use, transfer, clearance, settlement, or processing of:

(A) a deposit, loan, funds or monetary value represented in electronic form and stored or capable of storage electronically and retrievable and transferable electronically, or other right to payment to or from a person;

(B) an instrument or other item;

(C) a payment order, credit card transaction, debit card transaction, or a funds transfer, automated clearing house transfer, or similar wholesale or retail transfer of funds;

(D) a letter of credit, document of title, financial asset, investment property, or similar asset held in a fiduciary or agency capacity; or

(E) related identifying, verifying, access-enabling, authorizing, or monitoring information;

(5) is a contract for personal or entertainment services by an individual or group of individuals, other than a contract with an independent contractor to develop, support, modify, or maintain software;

(6) is a license for regularly scheduled audio or video programming by broadcast or cable as defined in the Federal Communications Act as that Act existed on January 1, 1998, or any similar regularly scheduled programming service;

(7) is a compulsory license under federal or state law;

(8) is a license of a linear motion picture or sound recording or of information to be included therein, except in connection with providing access to such motion picture or sound recording under an access contract covered by this article.

Default Rules

In general, the provisions of Article 2B are default rules. With some exceptions, the parties may agree to their own terms in lieu of the provisions of Article 2B. Application by "default" means that the parties did not consider the provision. In all cases, those provisions which cannot be varied by the parties will apply.

The License

The standard transaction for Article 2B is a license. The definition of a "license" under Article 2B is consistent with the common meaning of the term—i.e., a transfer of conditional or limited rights, not including a sale. However, the terms "licensee" and "licensor" used throughout the Article are expanded to include not just the parties to a license, but also any transferee and transferor, respectively, of rights under a contract governed by Article 2B.

Article 2 is insufficient to govern such licenses because contracts in information are not equivalent to transactions in goods. Under federal copyright law, computer software and most digital products are governed by intellectual property rights rules which provide that the copyright owner holds the "exclusive right to make copies, distribute copies, engage in public display or performances of the work, and to modify the work." This creates property rights much different from those associated with the sale of goods under Article 2.

Benefits Under Article 2B

As set forth in the Draft, a number of benefits are expected to flow from the adoption of UCC Article 2B.

General Benefits

Article 2B will:

Reduce uncertainty and non-uniformity of licensing law;

Create balanced structure for electronic contracting;

Confirm contract freedom in commercial transactions;

Provide contract law roadmap for converging industries;

Extend UCC contract formation rules to common law settings;

Innovate the concept of mass market transactions;

Enact strong protection for published informational content;

Set performance standards for Internet contracts;

Clarify enforceability of standard forms in commercial deals;

Clarify the obligation to mitigate damages;

Apply "material breach" concept for both parties;

Expand "good faith" to include commercial fair dealing;

Recognize layered contract formation occurring over time;

Establish contract law rules for idea submissions;

Adjust statute of frauds to information transactions;

Provide background rules for data processing and outsourcing contracts;

Define the relationships between retailer, publisher and end user;

Recognize contracts where rights vest before delivery of a copy;

Clarify when the title to a copy passes in a license;

Allow parties to contract for specific performance;

Refine the liquidated damages rule; and

Provide standard interpretations for grant terms.

Licensor Benefits

Article 2B will:

Create a workable method for contracting in the Internet;

Establish workable choice of law rules for the Internet;

Create workable contractual choice of forum rules;

Establish guidance for attribution in electronic contracts;

Settle enforceability of mass market licenses;

Exclude consequential damages for published informational content;

Clarify meaning and effect of subjective satisfaction terms;

Establish guidance on the meaning of license grants;

Establish reservation of title in a copy effective as to all copies made;

Deal with effect on warranty of modification of program code;

Codify contract treatment of electronic limiting devices;

Reconcile inspection with vulnerable confidential material;

Establish guidance on procedures to modify on-going contracts;

Confirm that exceeding a license is a breach of contract; and

Clarify the right to judicial repossession in licenses.

Licensee Benefits

Article 2B will:

Create cost-free refund right on refusal of mass market license;

Create procedural and substantive safeguards for mass- market contracts;

Create right of quiet enjoyment of a license;

Presume perpetual term in some licenses;

Codify that advertising can create express warranty;

Condition retailer's contract on approval of publisher's license;

Provide that retailer warranties are not disclaimed by the publisher license;

Create protection against errors for consumers in the Internet;

Create a warranty for data accuracy;

Expand implied warranties;

Create an implied system integration warranty;

Require disclaimers in a record (e.g., writing);

Create an implied license right;

Create early transfer of informational rights;

Enable financing without licensor consent;

Create a right to information about sources in a development contract;

Increase persons to whom warranties run for non-personal injury damage;

Enforce releases without consideration;

Provide for a longer statute of limitations;

Establish a discovery rule regarding limitation period for some claims;

Reject the theory that any failure to timely pay per se justifies cancellation;

Enforce term providing that a license cannot be canceled; and

Set out standards under contract for idea submissions.

Drafting Procedure

The drafting committee for Article 2B consists of the commissioners from the NCCUSL and representatives from The American Law Institute (ALI). Both NCCUSL and ALI must approve the final text. Under NCCUSL procedures, the proposed draft must be considered, section by section, at a minimum of two annual conferences. Once the NCCUSL conference, as a committee of the whole, has approved the draft, it must be approved by a majority of states present at the conference.

Article 2B is scheduled to go before the committee of the whole in November 1998. Once a final version is approved by both organizations, Article 2B will then be proposed to the states as a uniform law.

APPENDICES

APPENDIX 1:

APPLICABLE SECTIONS -
UCC ARTICLE 2 - SALES

SECTION 2-105. Definitions; Goods.

"Goods" means all things (including specially manufactured goods) which are movable at the time of identification to the contract for sale other than the money in which the price is to be paid, investment securities (Article 8) and things in action. "Goods" also includes the unborn young of animals and growing crops and other identified things attached to realty as described in the section on goods to be severed from realty.

SECTION 2-201. Formal Requirements; Statute of Frauds.

(1) Except as otherwise provided in this section a contract for the sale of goods for the price of $500 or more is not enforceable by way of action or defense unless there is some writing sufficient to indicate that a contract for sale has been made between the parties and signed by the party against whom enforcement is sought or by his authorized agent or broker. A writing is not insufficient because it omits or incorrectly states a term agreed upon but the contract is not enforceable under this paragraph beyond the quantity of goods shown in such writing.

(2) Between merchants if within a reasonable time a writing in confirmation of the contract and sufficient against the sender is received and the party receiving it has reason to know its contents, it satisfies the requirements of subsection (1) against such party unless written notice of objection to its contents is given within 10 days after it is received.

(3) A contract which does not satisfy the requirements of subsection (1) but which is valid in other respects is enforceable:

    (a) if the goods are to be specially manufactured for the buyer and are not suitable for sale to others in the ordinary course of the seller's business and the seller, before notice of repudiation is received and under circumstances which reasonably indicate that the goods are for the buyer, has made either a substantial beginning of their manufacture or commitments for their procurement; or

    (b) if the party against whom enforcement is sought admits in his pleading, testimony or otherwise in court that a contract for sale was made, but the contract is not enforceable under this provision beyond the quantity of goods admitted; or

(c) with respect to goods for which payment has been made and accepted or which have been received and accepted (Sec. 2-606).

SECTION 2-202. Final Written Expression: Parol or Extrinsic Evidence.

Terms with respect to which the confirmatory memoranda of the parties agree or which are otherwise set forth in a writing intended by the parties as a final expression of their agreement with respect to such terms as are included therein may not be contradicted by evidence of any prior agreement or of a contemporaneous oral agreement but may be explained or supplemented:

(a) by course of dealing or usage of trade (Section 1-205) or by course of performance (Section 2-208); and

(b) by evidence of consistent additional terms unless the court finds the writing to have been intended also as a complete and exclusive statement of the terms of the agreement .

SECTION 2-204. Formation in General.

(1) A contract for sale of goods may be made in any manner sufficient to show agreement, including conduct by both parties which recognizes the existence of such a contract.

(2) An agreement sufficient to constitute a contract for sale may be found even though the moment of its making is undetermined.

(3) Even though one or more terms are left open a contract for sale does not fail for indefiniteness if the parties have intended to make a contract and there is a reasonably certain basis for giving an appropriate remedy.

SECTION 2-205. Firm Offers.

An offer by a merchant to buy or sell goods in a signed writing which by its terms gives assurance that it will be held open is not revocable, for lack of consideration, during the time stated or if no time is stated for a reasonable time, but in no event may such period of irrevocability exceed three months; but any such term of assurance on a form supplied by the offeree must be separately signed by the offeror.

SECTION 2-206. Offer and Acceptance in Formation of Contract.

(1) Unless otherwise unambiguously indicated by the language or circumstances:

(a) an offer to make a contract shall be construed as inviting acceptance in any manner and by any medium reasonable in the circumstances;

(b) an order or other offer to buy goods for prompt or current shipment shall be construed as inviting acceptance either by a prompt promise to ship or by the prompt or current shipment of conforming or non-conforming goods, but such a shipment of non-conforming goods does not constitute an acceptance if the seller seasonably notifies the buyer that the shipment is offered only as an accommodation to the buyer.

(2) Where the beginning of a requested performance is a reasonable mode of acceptance an offeror who is not notified of acceptance within a reasonable time may treat the offer as having lapsed before acceptance.

SECTION 2-301. General Obligations of Parties.

The obligation of the seller is to transfer and deliver and that of the buyer is to accept and pay in accordance with the contract.

SECTION 2-302. Unconscionable contract or Clause.

(1) If the court as a matter of law finds the contract or any clause of the contract to have been unconscionable at the time it was made the court may refuse to enforce the contract, or it may enforce the remainder of the contract without the unconscionable clause, or it may so limit the application of any unconscionable clause as to avoid any unconscionable result.

(2) When it is claimed or appears to the court that the contract or any clause thereof may be unconscionable the parties shall be afforded a reasonable opportunity to present evidence as to its commercial setting, purpose and effect to aid the court in making the determination.

SECTION 2-306. Output, Requirements and Exclusive Dealings.

(1) A term which measures the quantity by the output of the seller or the requirements of the buyer means such actual output or requirements as may occur in good faith, except that no quantity unreasonably disproportionate to any stated estimate or in the absence of a stated estimate to any normal or otherwise comparable prior output or requirements may be tendered or demanded.

(2) A lawful agreement by either the seller or the buyer for exclusive dealing in the kind of goods concerned imposes unless otherwise agreed an obligation by the seller to use best efforts to supply the goods and by the buyer to use best efforts to promote their sale.

Unless otherwise agreed all goods called for by a contract for sale must be tendered in a single delivery and payment is due only on such tender but where the circumstances give either party the right to make or demand delivery in lots the price if it can be apportioned may be demanded for each lot.

SECTION 2-313. Express Warranties by Affirmation, Promise, Description, Sample.

(1) Express warranties by the seller are created as follows:

(a) Any affirmation of fact or promise made by the seller to the buyer which relates to the goods and becomes part of the basis of the bargain creates an express warranty that the goods shall conform to the affirmation or promise.

(b) Any description of the goods which is made part of the basis of the bargain creates an express warranty that the goods shall conform to the description.

(c) Any sample or model which is made part of the basis of the bargain creates an express warranty that the whole of the goods shall conform to the sample or model.

(2) It is not necessary to the creation of an express warranty that the seller use formal words such as "warrant" or "guarantee" or that he have a specific intention to make a warranty, but an affirmation merely of the value of the goods or a statement purporting to be merely the seller's opinion or commendation of the goods does not create a warranty.

SECTION 2-314. Implied Warranty: Merchantability; Usage of Trade.

(1) Unless excluded or modified (Section 2-316), a warranty that the goods shall be merchantable is implied in a contract for their sale if the seller is a merchant with respect to goods of that kind. Under this section the serving for value of food or drink to be consumed either on the premises or elsewhere is a sale.

(2) Goods to be merchantable must be at least such as

(a) pass without objection in the trade under the contract description; and

(b) in the case of fungible goods, are of fair average quality within the description; and

(c) are fit for the ordinary purposes for which such goods are used; and

(d) run, within the variations permitted by the agreement, of even kind, quality and quantity within each unit and among all units involved; and

(e) are adequately contained, packaged, and labeled as the agreement may require; and

(f) conform to the promise or affirmations of fact made on the container or label if any.

(3) Unless excluded or modified (Section 2-316) other implied warranties may arise from course of dealing or usage of trade.

SECTION 2-315. Implied Warranty: Fitness for Particular Purpose.

Where the seller at the time of contracting has reason to know any particular purpose for which the goods are required and that the buyer is relying on the seller's skill or judgment to select or furnish suitable goods, there is unless excluded or modified under the next section an implied warranty that the goods shall be fit for such purpose.

SECTION 2-319. F.O.B. and F.A.S. Terms.

(1) Unless otherwise agreed the term F.O.B. (which means "free on board") at a named place, even though used only in connection with the stated price, is a delivery term under which

(a) when the term is F.O.B. the place of shipment, the seller must at that place ship the goods in the manner provided in this Article (Section 2-504) and bear the expense and risk of putting them into the possession of the carrier; or

(b) when the term is F.O.B. the place of destination, the seller must at his own expense and risk transport the goods to that place and there tender delivery of them in the manner provided in this Article (Section 2-503);

(c) when under either (a) or (b) the term is also F.O.B. vessel, car or other vehicle, the seller must in addition at his own expense and risk load the goods on board. If the term is F.O.B. vessel the buyer must name the vessel and in an appropriate case the seller must comply with the provisions of this Article on the form of bill of lading (Section 2-323).

(2) Unless otherwise agreed the term F.A.S. vessel (which means "free alongside") at a named port, even though used only in connection with the stated price, is a delivery term under which the seller must

(a) at his own expense and risk deliver the goods alongside the vessel in the manner usual in that port or on a dock designated and provided by the buyer; and

(b) obtain and tender a receipt for the goods in exchange for which the carrier is under a duty to issue a bill of lading.

(3) Unless otherwise agreed in any case falling within subsection (1)(a) or (c) or subsection (2) the buyer must seasonably give any needed instructions for making delivery, including when the term is F.A.S. or F.O.B. the loading berth of the vessel and in an appropriate case its name and sailing date. The seller may treat the failure of needed instructions as a failure of co-operation under this Article (Section 2-311). He may also at his option move the goods in any reasonable manner preparatory to delivery or shipment.

(4) Under the term F.O.B. vessel or F.A.S. unless otherwise agreed the buyer must make payment against tender of the required documents and the seller may not tender nor the buyer demand delivery of the goods in substitution for the documents.

SECTION 2-320. C.I.F. and C. & F. Terms.

(1) The term C.I.F. means that the price includes in a lump sum the cost of the goods and the insurance and freight to the named destination. The term C. & F. or C.F. means that the price so includes cost and freight to the named destination.

(2) Unless otherwise agreed and even though used only in connection with the stated price and destination, the term C.I.F. destination or its equivalent requires the seller at his own expense and risk to

(a) put the goods into the possession of a carrier at the port for shipment and obtain a negotiable bill or bills of lading covering the entire transportation to the named destination; and

(b) load the goods and obtain a receipt from the carrier (which may be contained in the bill of lading) showing that the freight has been paid or provided for; and

(c) obtain a policy or certificate of insurance, including any war risk insurance, of a kind and on terms then current at the port of shipment in the usual amount, in the currency of the contract, shown to cover the same goods covered by the bill of lading and providing for payment of loss to the order of the buyer or for the account of whom it may concern; but the seller may add to the price the amount of the premium for any such war risk insurance; and

(d) prepare an invoice of the goods and procure any other documents required to effect shipment or to comply with the contract; and

(e) forward and tender with commercial promptness all the documents in due form and with any indorsement necessary to perfect the buyer's rights.

(3) Unless otherwise agreed the term C. & F. or its equivalent has the same effect and imposes upon the seller the same obligations and risks as a C.I.F. term except the obligation as to insurance.

(4) Under the term C.I.F. or C. & F. unless otherwise agreed the buyer must make payment against tender of the required documents and the seller may not tender nor the buyer demand delivery of the goods in substitution for the documents.

SECTION 2-703. Seller's Remedies in General

Where the buyer wrongfully rejects or revokes acceptance of goods or fails to make a payment due on or before delivery or repudiates with respect to a part or the whole, then with respect to any goods directly affected and, if the breach is of the whole contract, then also with respect to the whole undelivered balance, the aggrieved seller may:

(a) withhold delivery of such goods;

(b) stop delivery bay any bailee as hereafter provided (Section 2-705);

(c) proceed under the next section respecting goods still unidentified to the contract;

(d) resell and recovery damages as hereafter provided (Section 2-706);

(e) recover damages for non-acceptance (Section 2-708) or in a proper case the price (Section 2-709);

(f) cancel.

SECTION 2-706. Seller's Resale Including Contract for Resale.

(1) Under the conditions stated in Section 2-703 on seller's remedies, the seller may resell the goods concerned or the undelivered balance thereof. Where the resale is made in good faith and in a commercially reasonable manner the seller may recover the difference between the resale price and the contract price together with any incidental damages allowed under the provisions of this Article (Section 2-710), but less expenses saved in consequence of the buyer's breach.

SECTION 2-711. Buyer's Remedies in General; Buyer's Security Interest in Rejected Goods.

(1) Where the seller fails to make delivery or repudiates or the buyer rightfully rejects or justifiably revokes acceptance then with respect to any goods involved, and with respect to the whole if the breach goes to the whole contract (Section 2-612), the buyer may cancel and whether or not he has done so may in addition to recovering so much of the price as has been paid

(a) "cover" and have damages under the next section as to all the goods affected whether or not they have been identified to the contract; or

(b) recover damages for non-delivery as provided in this Article (Section 2-713).

(2) Where the seller fails to deliver or repudiates the buyer may also

(a) if the goods have been identified recover them as provided in this Article (Section 2-502); or

(b) in a proper case obtain specific performance or replevy the goods as provided in this Article (Section 2-716).

(3) On rightful rejection or justifiable revocation of acceptance a buyer has a security interest in goods in his possession or control for any payments made on their price and any expenses reasonably incurred in their inspection, receipt, transportation, care and custody and may hold such goods and resell them in like manner as an aggrieved seller (Section 2-706).

APPLICABLE SECTIONS -
UCC ARTICLE 2A - LEASES

SECTION 2A-102. SCOPE.

This Article applies to any transaction, regardless of form, that creates a lease.

SECTION 2A-108. UNCONSCIONABILITY.

(1) If the court as a matter of law finds a lease contract or any clause of a lease contract to have been unconscionable at the time it was made the court may refuse to enforce the lease contract, or it may enforce the remainder of the lease contract without the unconscionable clause, or it may so limit the application of any unconscionable clause as to avoid any unconscionable result.

(2) With respect to a consumer lease, if the court as a matter of law finds that a lease contract or any clause of a lease contract has been induced by unconscionable conduct or that unconscionable conduct has occurred in the collection of a claim arising from a lease contract, the court may grant appropriate relief.

(3) Before making a finding of unconscionability under subsection (1) or (2), the court, on its own motion or that of a party, shall afford the parties a reasonable opportunity to present evidence as to the setting, purpose, and effect of the lease contract or clause thereof, or of the conduct.

(4) In an action in which the lessee claims unconscionability with respect to a consumer lease:

(a) If the court finds unconscionability under subsection (1) or (2), the court shall award reasonable attorney's fees to the lessee.

(b) If the court does not find unconscionability and the lessee claiming unconscionability has brought or maintained an action he [or she] knew to be groundless, the court shall award reasonable attorney's fees to the party against whom the claim is made.

(c) In determining attorney's fees, the amount of the recovery on behalf of the claimant under subsections (1) and (2) is not controlling.

SECTION 2A-201. STATUTE OF FRAUDS.

(1) A lease contract is not enforceable by way of action or defense unless:

(a) the total payments to be made under the lease contract, excluding payments for options to renew or buy, are less than $1,000; or

(b) there is a writing, signed by the party against whom enforcement is sought or by that party's authorized agent, sufficient to indicate that a lease contract has been made between the parties and to describe the goods leased and the lease term.

(2) Any description of leased goods or of the lease term is sufficient and satisfies subsection (1)(b), whether or not it is specific, if it reasonably identifies what is described.

(3) A writing is not insufficient because it omits or incorrectly states a term agreed upon, but the lease contract is not enforceable under subsection (1)(b) beyond the lease term and the quantity of goods shown in the writing.

(4) A lease contract that does not satisfy the requirements of subsection (1), but which is valid in other respects, is enforceable:

(a) if the goods are to be specially manufactured or obtained for the lessee and are not suitable for lease or sale to others in the ordinary course of the lessor's business, and the lessor, before notice of repudiation is received and under circumstances that reasonably indicate that the goods are for the lessee, has made either a substantial beginning of their manufacture or commitments for their procurement;

(b) if the party against whom enforcement is sought admits in that party's pleading, testimony or otherwise in court that a lease contract was made, but the lease contract is not enforceable under this provision beyond the quantity of goods admitted; or

(c) with respect to goods that have been received and accepted by the lessee.

(5) The lease term under a lease contract referred to in subsection (4) is:

(a) if there is a writing signed by the party against whom enforcement is sought or by that party's authorized agent specifying the lease term, the term so specified;

(b) if the party against whom enforcement is sought admits in that party's pleading, testimony, or otherwise in court a lease term, the term so admitted; or

(c) a reasonable lease term.

SECTION 2A-202. FINAL WRITTEN EXPRESSION: PAROL OR EXTRINSIC EVIDENCE.

Terms with respect to which the confirmatory memoranda of the parties agree or which are otherwise set forth in a writing intended by the parties as a final expression of their agreement with respect to such terms as are included therein may not be contradicted by evidence of any prior agreement or of a contemporaneous oral agreement but may be explained or supplemented:

(a) by course of dealing or usage of trade or by course of performance; and

(b) by evidence of consistent additional terms unless the court finds the writing to have been intended also as a complete and exclusive statement of the terms of the agreement.

SECTION 2A-204. FORMATION IN GENERAL.

(1) A lease contract may be made in any manner sufficient to show agreement, including conduct by both parties which recognizes the existence of a lease contract.

(2) An agreement sufficient to constitute a lease contract may be found although the moment of its making is undetermined.

(3) Although one or more terms are left open, a lease contract does not fail for indefiniteness if the parties have intended to make a lease contract and there is a reasonably certain basis for giving an appropriate remedy.

SECTION 2A-205. FIRM OFFERS.

An offer by a merchant to lease goods to or from another person in a signed writing that by its terms gives assurance it will be held open is not revocable, for lack of consideration, during the time stated or, if no time is stated, for a reasonable time, but in no event may the period of irrevocability exceed 3 months. Any such term of assurance on a form supplied by the offeree must be separately signed by the offeror.

SECTION 2A-206. OFFER AND ACCEPTANCE IN FORMATION OF LEASE CONTRACT.

(1) Unless otherwise unambiguously indicated by the language or circumstances, an offer to make a lease contract must be construed as inviting acceptance in any manner and by any medium reasonable in the circumstances.

(2) If the beginning of a requested performance is a reasonable mode of acceptance, an offeror who is not notified of acceptance within a reasonable time may treat the offer as having lapsed before acceptance.

SECTION 2A-208. MODIFICATION, RESCISSION AND WAIVER.

(1) An agreement modifying a lease contract needs no consideration to be binding.

(2) A signed lease agreement that excludes modification or rescission except by a signed writing may not be otherwise modified or rescinded, but, except as between merchants, such a requirement on a form supplied by a merchant must be separately signed by the other party.

(3) Although an attempt at modification or rescission does not satisfy the requirements of subsection (2), it may operate as a waiver.

(4) A party who has made a waiver affecting an executory portion of a lease contract may retract the waiver by reasonable notification received by the other party that strict performance will be required of any term waived, unless the retraction would be unjust in view of a material change of position in reliance on the waiver.

SECTION 2A-210. EXPRESS WARRANTIES.

(1) Express warranties by the lessor are created as follows:

Any affirmation of fact or promise made by the lessor to the lessee which relates to the goods and becomes part of the basis of the bargain creates an express warranty that the goods will conform to the affirmation or promise.

(b) Any description of the goods which is made part of the basis of the bargain creates an express warranty that the goods will conform to the description.

(c) Any sample or model that is made part of the basis of the bargain creates an express warranty that the whole of the goods will conform to the sample or model.

(2) It is not necessary to the creation of an express warranty that the lessor use formal words, such as "warrant" or "guarantee," or that the lessor have a specific intention to make a warranty, but an affirmation merely of the value of the goods or a statement purporting to be merely the lessor's opinion or commendation of the goods does not create a warranty.

SECTION 2A-211. WARRANTIES AGAINST INTERFERENCE AND AGAINST INFRINGEMENT; LESSEE'S OBLIGATION AGAINST INFRINGEMENT.

(1) There is in a lease contract a warranty that for the lease term no person holds a claim to or interest in the goods that arose from an act or omission of the lessor, other than a claim by way of infringement or the like, which will interfere with the lessee's enjoyment of its leasehold interest.

(2) Except in a finance lease there is in a lease contract by a lessor who is a merchant regularly dealing in goods of the kind a warranty that the goods are delivered free of the rightful claim of any person by way of infringement or the like.

(3) A lessee who furnishes specifications to a lessor or a supplier shall hold the lessor and the supplier harmless against any claim by way of infringement or the like that arises out of compliance with the specifications.

SECTION 2A-212. IMPLIED WARRANTY OF MERCHANTABILITY.

(1) Except in a finance lease, a warranty that the goods will be merchantable is implied in a lease contract if the lessor is a merchant with respect to goods of that kind.

(2) Goods to be merchantable must be at least such as

(a) pass without objection in the trade under the description in the lease agreement;

(b) in the case of fungible goods, are of fair average quality within the description;

(c) are fit for the ordinary purposes for which goods of that type are used;

(d) run, within the variation permitted by the lease agreement, of even kind, quality, and quantity within each unit and among all units involved;

(e) are adequately contained, packaged, and labeled as the lease agreement may require; and

(f) conform to any promises or affirmations of fact made on the container or label.

(3) Other implied warranties may arise from course of dealing or usage of trade.

SECTION 2A-213. IMPLIED WARRANTY OF FITNESS FOR PARTICULAR PURPOSE.

Except in a finance lease, if the lessor at the time the lease contract is made has reason to know of any particular purpose for which the goods are required and that the lessee is relying on the lessor's skill or judgment to select or furnish suitable goods, there is in the lease contract an implied warranty that the goods will be fit for that purpose.

SECTION 2A-301. ENFORCEABILITY OF LEASE CONTRACT.

Except as otherwise provided in this Article, a lease contract is effective and enforceable according to its terms between the parties, against purchasers of the goods and against creditors of the parties.

APPENDIX 3:

APPLICABLE SECTIONS -
UCC ARTICLE 3 - NEGOTIABLE INSTRUMENTS

SECTION 3-108. PAYABLE ON DEMAND OR AT DEFINITE TIME

(a) A promise or order is "payable on demand" if it (i) states that it is payable on demand or at sight, or otherwise indicates that it is payable at the will of the holder, or (ii) does not state any time of payment.

(b) A promise or order is "payable at a definite time" if it is payable on elapse of a definite period of time after sight or acceptance or at a fixed date or dates or at a time or times readily ascertainable at the time the promise or order is issued, subject to rights of (i) prepayment, (ii) acceleration, (iii) extension at the option of the holder, or (iv) extension to a further definite time at the option of the maker or acceptor or automatically upon or after a specified act or event.

(c) If an instrument, payable at a fixed date, is also payable upon demand made before the fixed date, the instrument is payable on demand until the fixed date and, if demand for payment is not made before that date, becomes payable at a definite time on the fixed date.

SECTION 3-109. PAYABLE TO BEARER OR TO ORDER

(a) A promise or order is payable to bearer if it:

(1) states that it is payable to bearer or to the order of bearer or otherwise indicates that the person in possession of the promise or order is entitled to payment;

(2) does not state a payee; or

(3) states that it is payable to or to the order of cash or otherwise indicates that it is not payable to an identified person.

(b) A promise or order that is not payable to bearer is payable to order if it is payable (i) to the order of an identified person or (ii) to an identified person or order. A promise or order that is payable to order is payable to the identified person.

(c) An instrument payable to bearer may become payable to an identified person if it is specially indorsed pursuant to Section 3-205(a). An instrument payable to an identified person may become payable to bearer if it is indorsed in blank pursuant to Section 3-205(b).

SECTION 3-205. SPECIAL INDORSEMENT; BLANK INDORSEMENT; ANOMALOUS INDORSEMENT

(a) If an indorsement is made by the holder of an instrument, whether payable to an identified person or payable to bearer, and the indorsement identifies a person to whom it makes the instrument payable, it is a "special indorsement." When specially indorsed, an instrument becomes payable to the identified person and may be negotiated only by the indorsement of that person. The principles stated in Section 3-110 apply to special indorsements.

(b) If an indorsement is made by the holder of an instrument and it is not a special indorsement, it is a "blank indorsement." When indorsed in blank, an instrument becomes payable to bearer and may be negotiated by transfer of possession alone until specially indorsed.

SECTION 3-302. HOLDER IN DUE COURSE

(a) Subject to subsection (c) and Section 3-106(d), "holder in due course" means the holder of an instrument if:

(1) the instrument when issued or negotiated to the holder does not bear such apparent evidence of forgery or alteration or is not otherwise so irregular or incomplete as to call into question its authenticity; and

(2) the holder took the instrument (i) for value, (ii) in good faith, (iii) without notice that the instrument is overdue or has been dishonored or that there is an uncured default with respect to payment of another instrument issued as part of the same series, (iv) without notice that the instrument contains an unauthorized signature or has been altered, (v) without notice of any claim to the instrument described in Section 3-306, and (vi) without notice that any party has a defense or claim in recoupment described in Section 3-305(a).

SECTION 3-305. DEFENSES AND CLAIMS IN RECOUPMENT.

(a) [T]he right to enforce the obligation of a party to pay an instrument is subject to the following:

(1) a defense of the obligor based on (i) infancy of the obligor to the extent it is a defense to a simple contract, (ii) duress, lack of legal capacity, or illegality of the transaction which, under other law, nullifies the obligation of the obligor, (iii) fraud that induced the obligor to sign the instrument with neither knowledge nor reasonable opportunity to learn of its character or its essential terms, or (iv) discharge of the obligor in insolvency proceedings.

SECTION 3-401. SIGNATURE

(a) A person is not liable on an instrument unless (i) the person signed the instrument, or (ii) the person is represented by an agent or representative who signed the instrument and the signature is binding on the represented person under Section 3-402.

SECTION 3-402. SIGNATURE BY REPRESENTATIVE

(a) If a person acting, or purporting to act, as a representative signs an instrument by signing either the name of the represented person or the name of the signer, the represented person is bound by the signature to the same extent the represented person would be bound if the signature were on a simple contract. If the represented person is bound, the signature of the representative is the "authorized signature of the represented person" and the represented person is liable on the instrument, whether or not identified in the instrument.

(b) If a representative signs the name of the representative to an instrument and the signature is an authorized signature of the represented person, the following rules apply:

(1) If the form of the signature shows unambiguously that the signature is made on behalf of the represented person who is identified in the instrument, the representative is not liable on the instrument.

(2) Subject to subsection (c), if (i) the form of the signature does not show unambiguously that the signature is made in a representative capacity or (ii) the represented person is not identified in the instrument, the representative is liable on the instrument to a holder in due course that took the instrument without notice that the representative was not intended to be liable on the instrument. With respect to any other person, the representative is liable on the instrument unless the representative proves that the original parties did not intend the representative to be liable on the instrument.

(c) If a representative signs the name of the representative as drawer of a check without indication of the representative status and the check is payable from an account of the represented person who is identified on the check, the signer is not liable on the check if the signature is an authorized signature of the represented person.

SECTION 3-403. UNAUTHORIZED SIGNATURE

(a) Unless otherwise provided in this Article or Article 4, an unauthorized signature is ineffective except as the signature of the unauthorized signer in favor of a person who in good faith pays the instrument or takes it for value. An unauthorized signature may be ratified for all purposes of this Article.

SECTION 3-416. TRANSFER WARRANTIES

(a) A person who transfers an instrument for consideration warrants to the transferee and, if the transfer is by indorsement, to any subsequent transferee that:

(1) the warrantor is a person entitled to enforce the instrument;

(2) all signatures on the instrument are authentic and authorized;

(3) the instrument has not been altered;

(4) the instrument is not subject to a defense or claim in recoupment of any party which can be asserted against the warrantor; and

(5) the warrantor has no knowledge of any insolvency proceeding commenced with respect to the maker or acceptor or, in the case of an unaccepted draft, the drawer.

(b) A person to whom the warranties under subsection (a) are made and who took the instrument in good faith may recover from the warrantor as damages for breach of warranty an amount equal to the loss suffered as a result of the breach, but not more than the amount of the instrument plus expenses and loss of interest incurred as a result of the breach.

SECTION 3-601. DISCHARGE AND EFFECT OF DISCHARGE

(a) The obligation of a party to pay the instrument is discharged as stated in this Article or by an act or agreement with the party which would discharge an obligation to pay money under a simple contract.

(b) Discharge of the obligation of a party is not effective against a person acquiring rights of a holder in due course of the instrument without notice of the discharge.

SECTION 3-602. PAYMENT

(a) Subject to subsection (b), an instrument is paid to the extent payment is made (i) by or on behalf of a party obliged to pay the instrument, and (ii) to a person entitled to enforce the instrument. To the extent of the payment, the obligation of the party obliged to pay the instrument is discharged even though payment is made with knowledge of a claim to the instrument under Section 3-306 by another person.

(b) The obligation of a party to pay the instrument is not discharged under subsection (a) if:

(1) a claim to the instrument under Section 3-306 is enforceable against the party receiving payment and (I) payment is made with knowledge by the payor that payment is prohibited by injunction or similar process of a court of competent jurisdiction, or (ii) in the case of an instrument other than a cashier's check, teller's check, or certified check, the party making payment accepted, from the person having a claim to the instrument, indemnity against loss resulting from refusal to pay the person entitled to enforce the instrument; or

(2) the person making payment knows that the instrument is a stolen instrument and pays a person it knows is in wrongful possession of the instrument.

SECTION 3-604. DISCHARGE BY CANCELLATION OR RENUNCIATION

(a) A person entitled to enforce an instrument, with or without consideration, may discharge the obligation of a party to pay the instrument (i) by an intentional voluntary act, such as surrender of the instrument to the party, destruction, mutilation, or cancellation of the instrument, cancellation or striking out of the party's signature, or the addition of words to the instrument indicating discharge, or (ii) by agreeing not to sue or otherwise renouncing rights against the party by a signed writing.

APPENDIX 4:

APPLICABLE SECTIONS -
UCC ARTICLE 4 - BANK DEPOSITS AND COLLECTIONS

SECTION 4-201. STATUS OF COLLECTING BANK AS AGENT AND PROVISIONAL STATUS OF CREDITS

(a) Unless a contrary intent clearly appears and before the time that a settlement given by a collecting bank for an item is or becomes final, the bank, with respect to the item, is an agent or sub-agent of the owner of the item and any settlement given for the item is provisional . . .

SECTION 4-202. RESPONSIBILITY FOR COLLECTION OR RETURN; WHEN ACTION TIMELY

(a) A collecting bank must exercise ordinary care in:

(1) presenting an item or sending it for presentment;

(2) sending notice of dishonor or nonpayment or returning an item other than a documentary draft to the bank's transferor after learning that the item has not been paid or accepted, as the case may be;

(3) settling for an item when the bank receives final settlement; and

(4) notifying its transferor of any loss or delay in transit within a reasonable time after discovery thereof.

(b) A collecting bank exercises ordinary care under subsection (a) by taking proper action before its midnight deadline following receipt of an item, notice, or settlement. Taking proper action within a reasonably longer time may constitute the exercise of ordinary care, but the bank has the burden of establishing timeliness.

SECTION 4-205. DEPOSITARY BANK HOLDER OF UNINDORSED ITEM

If a customer delivers an item to a depositary bank for collection:

(1) the depositary bank becomes a holder of the item at the time it receives the item for collection if the customer at the time of delivery was a holder of the item, whether or not the customer indorses the item, and, if the bank satisfies the other requirements of Section 3-302, it is a holder in due course; and

(2) the depositary bank warrants to collecting banks, the payor bank or other payor, and the drawer that the amount of the item was paid to the customer or deposited to the customer's account.

SECTION 4-207. TRANSFER WARRANTIES

(a) A customer or collecting bank that transfers an item and receives a settlement or other consideration warrants to the transferee and to any subsequent collecting bank that:

(1) the warrantor is a person entitled to enforce the item;

(2) all signatures on the item are authentic and authorized;

(3) the item has not been altered;

(4) the item is not subject to a defense or claim in recoupment (Section 3-305(a)) of any party that can be asserted against the warrantor; and

(5) the warrantor has no knowledge of any insolvency proceeding commenced with respect to the maker or acceptor or, in the case of an unaccepted draft, the drawer.

(b) If an item is dishonored, a customer or collecting bank transferring the item and receiving settlement or other consideration is obliged to pay the amount due on the item (i) according to the terms of the item at the time it was transferred, or (ii) if the transfer was of an incomplete item, according to its terms when completed as stated in Sections 3-115 and 3-407. The obligation of a transferor is owed to the transferee and to any subsequent collecting bank that takes the item in good faith. A transferor cannot disclaim its obligation under this subsection by an indorsement stating that it is made "without recourse" or otherwise disclaiming liability.

(c) A person to whom the warranties under subsection (a) are made and who took the item in good faith may recover from the warrantor as damages for breach of warranty an amount equal to the loss suffered as a result of the breach, but not more than the amount of the item plus expenses and loss of interest incurred as a result of the breach.

(d) The warranties stated in subsection (a) cannot be disclaimed with respect to checks. Unless notice of a claim for breach of warranty is given to the warrantor within 30 days after the claimant has reason to know of the breach and the identity of the warrantor, the warrantor is discharged to the extent of any loss caused by the delay in giving notice of the claim.

(e) A cause of action for breach of warranty under this section accrues when the claimant has reason to know of the breach.

SECTION 4-208. PRESENTMENT WARRANTIES

(a) If an unaccepted draft is presented to the drawee for payment or acceptance and the drawee pays or accepts the draft, (i) the person obtaining payment or acceptance, at the time of presentment, and (ii) a previous transferor of the draft, at the time of transfer, warrant to the drawee that pays or accepts the draft in good faith that:

(1) the warrantor is, or was, at the time the warrantor transferred the draft, a person entitled to enforce the draft or authorized to obtain payment or acceptance of the draft on behalf of a person entitled to enforce the draft;

(2) the draft has not been altered; and

(3) the warrantor has no knowledge that the signature of the purported drawer of the draft is unauthorized.

(b) A drawee making payment may recover from a warrantor damages for breach of warranty equal to the amount paid by the drawee less the amount the drawee received or is entitled to receive from the drawer because of the payment. In addition, the drawee is entitled to compensation for expenses and loss of interest resulting from the breach...

SECTION 4-401. WHEN BANK MAY CHARGE CUSTOMER'S ACCOUNT

(a) A bank may charge against the account of a customer an item that is properly payable from that account even though the charge creates an overdraft. An item is properly payable if it is authorized by the customer and is in accordance with any agreement between the customer and bank.

(b) A customer is not liable for the amount of an overdraft if the customer neither signed the item nor benefitted from the proceeds of the item.

(c) A bank may charge against the account of a customer a check that is otherwise properly payable from the account, even though payment was made before the date of the check, unless the customer has given notice to the bank of the postdating describing the check with reasonable certainty. The notice is effective for the period stated in Section 4-403(b) for stop-payment orders, and must be received at such time and in such manner as to afford the bank a reasonable opportunity to act on it before the bank takes any action with respect to the check described in Section 4-303. If a bank charges against the account of a customer a check before the date stated in the notice of postdating, the bank is liable for damages for the loss resulting from its act. The loss may include damages for dishonor of subsequent items under Section 4-402.

(d) A bank that in good faith makes payment to a holder may charge the indicated account of its customer according to:

(1) the original terms of the altered item; or

(2) the terms of the completed item, even though the bank knows the item has been completed unless the bank has notice that the completion was improper.

SECTION 4-403. CUSTOMER'S RIGHT TO STOP PAYMENT; BURDEN OF PROOF OF LOSS

(a) A customer or any person authorized to draw on the account if there is more than one person may stop payment of any item drawn on the customer's account or close the account by an order to the bank describing the item or account with reasonable certainty received at a time and in a manner that affords the bank a reasonable opportunity to act on it before any action by the bank with respect to the item described in Section 4-303. If the signature of more than one person is required to draw on an account, any of these persons may stop payment or close the account.

(b) A stop-payment order is effective for six months, but it lapses after 14 calendar days if the original order was oral and was not confirmed in writing within that period. A stop- payment order may be renewed for additional six-month periods by a writing given to the bank within a period during which the stop-payment order is effective.

SECTION 4-404. BANK NOT OBLIGED TO PAY CHECK MORE THAN SIX MONTHS OLD

A bank is under no obligation to a customer having a checking account to pay a check, other than a certified check, which is presented more than six months after its date, but it may charge its customer's account for a payment made thereafter in good faith.

SECTION 4-503. RESPONSIBILITY OF PRESENTING BANK FOR DOCUMENTS AND GOODS; REPORT OF REASONS FOR DISHONOR; REFEREE IN CASE OF NEED.

Unless otherwise instructed and except as provided in Article 5, a bank presenting a documentary draft:

(1) must deliver the documents to the drawee on acceptance of the draft if it is payable more than three days after presentment; otherwise, only on payment; and

(2) upon dishonor, either in the case of presentment for acceptance or presentment for payment, may seek and follow instructions from any referee in case of need designated in the draft or, if the presenting bank does not choose to utilize the referee's services, it must use diligence and good faith to ascertain the reason for dishonor, must notify its transferor of the dishonor and of the results of its effort to ascertain the reasons therefor, and must request instructions . . .

APPENDIX 5:

APPLICABLE SECTIONS - UCC ARTICLE 4A - FUNDS TRANSFERS

SECTION 4A-201. SECURITY PROCEDURE

"Security procedure" means a procedure established by agreement of a customer and a receiving bank for the purpose of (i) verifying that a payment order or communication amending or canceling a payment order is that of the customer, or (ii) detecting error in the transmission or the content of the payment order or communication. A security procedure may require the use of algorithms or other codes, identifying words or numbers, encryption, callback procedures, or similar security devices. Comparison of a signature on a payment order or communication with an authorized specimen signature of the customer is not by itself a security procedure.

SECTION 4A-202. AUTHORIZED AND VERIFIED PAYMENT ORDERS

(b) If a bank and its customer have agreed that the authenticity of payment orders issued to the bank in the name of the customer as sender will be verified pursuant to a security procedure, a payment order received by the receiving bank is effective as the order of the customer, whether or not authorized, if (i) the security procedure is a commercially reasonable method of providing security against unauthorized payment orders, and (ii) the bank proves that it accepted the payment order in good faith and in compliance with the security procedure and any written agreement or instruction of the customer restricting acceptance of payment orders issued in the name of the customer. The bank is not required to follow an instruction that violates a written agreement with the customer or notice of which is not received at a time and in a manner affording the bank a reasonable opportunity to act on it before the payment order is accepted.

SECTION 4A-203. UNENFORCEABILITY OF CERTAIN VERIFIED PAYMENT ORDERS

(a) If an accepted payment order is not, under Section 4A-202(a), an authorized order of a customer identified as sender, but is effective as an order of the customer pursuant to Section 4A-202(b):

(2) The receiving bank is not entitled to enforce or retain payment of the payment order if the customer proves that the order was not caused, directly or indirectly, by a person (i) entrusted at any time with duties to

act for the customer with respect to payment orders or the security procedure, or (ii) who obtained access to transmitting facilities of the customer or who obtained, from a source controlled by the customer and without authority of the receiving bank, information facilitating breach of the security procedure, regardless of how the information was obtained or whether the customer was at fault. Information includes any access device, computer software, or the like.

SECTION 4A-207. MISDESCRIPTION OF BENEFICIARY.

(a) Subject to subsection (b), if, in a payment order received by the beneficiary's bank, the name, bank account number, or other identification of the beneficiary refers to a nonexistent or unidentifiable person or account, no person has rights as a beneficiary of the order and acceptance of the order cannot occur.

(b) If a payment order received by the beneficiary's bank identifies the beneficiary both by name and by an identifying or bank account number and the name and number identify different persons, the following rules apply:

(1) Except as otherwise provided in subsection (c), if the beneficiary's bank does not know that the name and number refer to different persons, it may rely on the number as the proper identification of the beneficiary of the order. The beneficiary's bank need not determine whether the name and number refer to the same person.

(2) If the beneficiary's bank pays the person identified by name or knows that the name and number identify different persons, no person has rights as beneficiary except the person paid by the beneficiary's bank if that person was entitled to receive payment from the originator of the funds transfer. If no person has rights as beneficiary, acceptance of the order cannot occur.

(c) If (i) a payment order described in subsection (b) is accepted, (ii) the originator's payment order described the beneficiary inconsistently by name and number, and (iii) the beneficiary's bank pays the person identified by number as permitted by subsection (b)(1), the following rules apply:

(1) If the originator is a bank, the originator is obliged to pay its order.

(2) If the originator is not a bank and proves that the person identified by number was not entitled to receive payment from the originator, the originator is not obliged to pay its order unless the originator's bank proves that the originator, before acceptance of the originator's order, had notice that payment of a payment order issued by the originator might be made by the beneficiary's bank on the basis of an identifying or

bank account number even if it identifies a person different from the named beneficiary. Proof of notice may be made by any admissible evidence. The originator's bank satisfies the burden of proof if it proves that the originator, before the payment order was accepted, signed a writing stating the information to which the notice relates.

(d) In a case governed by subsection (b)(1), if the beneficiary's bank rightfully pays the person identified by number and that person was not entitled to receive payment from the originator, the amount paid may be recovered from that person to the extent allowed by the law governing mistake and restitution as follows:

(1) If the originator is obliged to pay its payment order as stated in subsection (c), the originator has the right to recover.

(2) If the originator is not a bank and is not obliged to pay its payment order, the originator's bank has the right to recover.

SECTION 4A-209. ACCEPTANCE OF PAYMENT ORDER

(a) Subject to subsection (d), a receiving bank other than the beneficiary's bank accepts a payment order when it executes the order.

(b) Subject to subsections (c) and (d), a beneficiary's bank accepts a payment order at the earliest of the following times:

(1) when the bank (i) pays the beneficiary as stated in Section 4A-405(a) or 4A-405(b), or (ii) notifies the beneficiary of receipt of the order or that the account of the beneficiary has been credited with respect to the order unless the notice indicates that the bank is rejecting the order or that funds with respect to the order may not be withdrawn or used until receipt of payment from the sender of the order;

(2) when the bank receives payment of the entire amount of the sender's order pursuant to Section 4A-403(a)(1) or 4A-403(a)(2); or

(3) the opening of the next funds-transfer business day of the bank following the payment date of the order if, at that time, the amount of the sender's order is fully covered by a withdrawable credit balance in an authorized account of the sender or the bank has otherwise received full payment from the sender, unless the order was rejected before that time or is rejected within (i) one hour after that time, or (ii) one hour after the opening of the next business day of the sender following the payment date if that time is later. If notice of rejection is received by the sender after the payment date and the authorized account of the sender does not bear interest, the bank is obliged to pay interest to the sender on the amount of the order for the number of days elapsing after the payment

date to the day the sender receives notice or learns that the order was not accepted, counting that day as an elapsed day. If the withdrawable credit balance during that period falls below the amount of the order, the amount of interest payable is reduced accordingly.

(c) Acceptance of a payment order cannot occur before the order is received by the receiving bank. Acceptance does not occur under subsection (b)(2) or (b)(3) if the beneficiary of the payment order does not have an account with the receiving bank, the account has been closed, or the receiving bank is not permitted by law to receive credits for the beneficiary's account.

(d) A payment order issued to the originator's bank cannot be accepted until the payment date if the bank is the beneficiary's bank, or the execution date if the bank is not the beneficiary's bank. If the originator's bank executes the originator's payment order before the execution date or pays the beneficiary of the originator's payment order before the payment date and the payment order is subsequently canceled pursuant to Section 4A-211(b), the bank may recover from the beneficiary any payment received to the extent allowed by the law governing mistake and restitution.

SECTION 4A-210. REJECTION OF PAYMENT ORDER

(a) A payment order is rejected by the receiving bank by a notice of rejection transmitted to the sender orally, electronically, or in writing. A notice of rejection need not use any particular words and is sufficient if it indicates that the receiving bank is rejecting the order or will not execute or pay the order. Rejection is effective when the notice is given if transmission is by a means that is reasonable in the circumstances. If notice of rejection is given by a means that is not reasonable, rejection is effective when the notice is received. If an agreement of the sender and receiving bank establishes the means to be used to reject a payment order, (i) any means complying with the agreement is reasonable and (ii) any means not complying is not reasonable unless no significant delay in receipt of the notice resulted from the use of the noncomplying means.

SECTION 4A-211. CANCELLATION AND AMENDMENT OF PAYMENT ORDER

(a) A communication of the sender of a payment order canceling or amending the order may be transmitted to the receiving bank orally, electronically, or in writing. If a security procedure is in effect between the sender and the receiving bank, the communication is not effective to cancel or amend the order unless the communication is verified pursuant to the security procedure or the bank agrees to the cancellation or amendment.

(b) Subject to subsection (a), a communication by the sender canceling or amending a payment order is effective to cancel or amend the order if notice of the communication is received at a time and in a manner affording the receiving bank a reasonable opportunity to act on the communication before the bank accepts the payment order.

(c) After a payment order has been accepted, cancellation or amendment of the order is not effective unless the receiving bank agrees or a funds-transfer system rule allows cancellation or amendment without agreement of the bank.

SECTION 4A-401. PAYMENT DATE

"Payment date" of a payment order means the day on which the amount of the order is payable to the beneficiary by the beneficiary's bank. The payment date may be determined by instruction of the sender but cannot be earlier than the day the order is received by the beneficiary's bank and, unless otherwise determined, is the day the order is received by the beneficiary's bank.

SECTION 4A-402. OBLIGATION OF SENDER TO PAY RECEIVING BANK.

(a) This section is subject to Sections 4A-205 and 4A-207.

(b) With respect to a payment order issued to the beneficiary's bank, acceptance of the order by the bank obliges the sender to pay the bank the amount of the order, but payment is not due until the payment date of the order.

(c) This subsection is subject to subsection (e) and to Section 4A-303. With respect to a payment order issued to a receiving bank other than the beneficiary's bank, acceptance of the order by the receiving bank obliges the sender to pay the bank the amount of the sender's order. Payment by the sender is not due until the execution date of the sender's order. The obligation of that sender to pay its payment order is excused if the funds transfer is not completed by acceptance by the beneficiary's bank of a payment order instructing payment to the beneficiary of that sender's payment order.

SECTION 4A-405. PAYMENT BY BENEFICIARY'S BANK TO BENEFICIARY

(a) If the beneficiary's bank credits an account of the beneficiary of a payment order, payment of the bank's obligation under Section 4A-404(a) occurs when and to the extent (i) the beneficiary is notified of the right to withdraw the credit, (ii) the bank lawfully applies the credit to a debt of the beneficiary, or (iii) funds with respect to the order are otherwise made available to the beneficiary by the bank.

APPENDIX 6:

APPLICABLE SECTIONS -
UCC ARTICLE 5 - LETTERS OF CREDIT

SECTION 5-104. FORMAL REQUIREMENTS; SIGNING

(1) Except as otherwise required in subsection (1)(c) of Section 5-102 on scope, no particular form of phrasing is required for a credit. A credit must be in writing and signed by the issuer and a confirmation must be in writing and signed by the confirming bank. A modification of the terms of a credit or confirmation must be signed by the issuer or confirming bank.

SECTION 5-106. TIME AND EFFECT OF ESTABLISHMENT OF CREDIT

(1) Unless otherwise agreed a credit is established

(a) as regards the customer as soon as a letter of credit is sent to him or the letter of credit or an authorized written advice of its issuance is sent to the beneficiary; and

(b) as regards the beneficiary when he receives a letter of credit or an authorized written advice of its issuance.

(2) Unless otherwise agreed once an irrevocable credit is established as regards the customer it can be modified or revoked only with the consent of the customer and once it is established as regards the beneficiary it can be modified or revoked only with his consent.

SECTION 5-107. ADVICE OF CREDIT; CONFIRMATION; ERROR IN STATEMENT TERMS

(1) Unless otherwise specified an advising bank by advising a credit issued by another bank does not assume any obligation to honor drafts drawn or demands for payment made under the credit but it does assume obligation for the accuracy of its own statement.

(2) A confirming bank by confirming a credit becomes directly obligated on the credit to the extent of its confirmation as though it were its issuer and acquires the rights of an issuer.

ties that the necessary conditions of the credit have been complied with. This is in addition to any warranties arising under Articles 3, 4, 7 and 8.

SECTION 5-114. ISSUER'S DUTY AND PRIVILEGE TO HONOR; RIGHT TO REIMBURSEMENT

(1) An issuer must honor a draft or demand for payment which complies with the terms of the relevant credit regardless of whether the goods or documents conform to the underlying contract for sale or other contract between the customer and the beneficiary. The issuer is not excused from honor of such a draft or demand by reason of an additional general term that all documents must be satisfactory to the issuer, but an issuer may require that specified documents must be satisfactory to it.

SECTION 5-115. REMEDY FOR IMPROPER DISHONOR OR ANTICIPATORY REPUDIATION

(1) When an issuer wrongfully dishonors a draft or demand for payment presented under a credit the person entitled to honor has with respect to any documents the rights of a person in the position of a seller (Section 2-707) and may recover from the issuer the face amount of the draft or demand together with incidental damages under Section 2-710 on seller's incidental damages and interest but less any amount realized by resale or other use or disposition of the subject matter of the transaction. In the event no resale or other utilization is made the documents, goods or other subject matter involved in the transaction must be turned over to the issuer on payment of judgment.

(2) When an issuer wrongfully cancels or otherwise repudiates a credit before presentment of a draft or demand for payment drawn under it the beneficiary has the rights of a seller after anticipatory repudiation by the buyer under Section 2-610 if he learns of the repudiation in time reasonably to avoid procurement of the required documents. Otherwise the beneficiary has an immediate right of action for wrongful dishonor.

APPENDIX 7:

APPLICABLE SECTIONS -
UCC ARTICLE 6 - BULK SALES

SECTION 6-103. APPLICABILITY OF ARTICLE

(1) Except as otherwise provided in subsection (3), this Article applies to a bulk sale if:

(a) the seller's principal business is the sale of inventory from stock; and

(b) on the date of the bulk-sale agreement the seller is located in this state or, if the seller is located in a jurisdiction that is not a part of the United States, the seller's major executive office in the United States is in this state.

(3) This article does not apply to . . . (l) a sale of assets having:

(i) a value, net of liens and security interests, of less than $10,000. If a debt is secured by assets and other property of the seller, the net value of the assets is determined by subtracting from their value an amount equal to the product of the debt multiplied by a fraction, the numerator of which is the value of the assets on the date of the bulk sale and the denominator of which is the value of all property securing the debt on the date of the bulk sale; or

(ii) a value of more than $25,000,000 on the date of the bulk-sale agreement.

SECTION 6-104. OBLIGATIONS OF BUYER

(1) In a bulk sale as defined in Section 6-102(1)(c)(ii) the buyer shall:

(a) obtain from the seller a list of all business names and addresses used by the seller within three years before the date the list is sent or delivered to the buyer;

(b) unless excused under subsection (2), obtain from the seller a verified and dated list of claimants of whom the seller has notice three days before the seller sends or delivers the list to the buyer and including, to the extent known by the seller, the address of and the amount claimed by each claimant;

(c) obtain from the seller or prepare a schedule of distribution (Section 6-106(1));

(d) give notice of the bulk sale in accordance with Section 6-105;

(e) unless excused under Section 6-106(4), distribute the net contract price in accordance with the undertakings of the buyer in the schedule of distribution; and

(f) unless excused under subsection (2), make available the list of claimants (subsection (1)(b)) by:

(i) promptly sending or delivering a copy of the list without charge to any claimant whose written request is received by the buyer no later than six months after the date of the bulk sale;

(ii) permitting any claimant to inspect and copy the list at any reasonable hour upon request received by the buyer no later than six months after the date of the bulk sale; or

(iii) filing a copy of the list in the office of the [Secretary of State] no later than the time for giving a notice of the bulk sale (Section 6-105(5)). A list filed in accordance with this subparagraph must state the individual, partnership, or corporate name and a mailing address of the seller.

(2) A buyer who gives notice in accordance with Section 6-105(2) is excused from complying with the requirements of subsections (1)(b) and (1)(f).

SECTION 6-107. LIABILITY FOR NONCOMPLIANCE

(1) Except as provided in subsection (3), and subject to the limitation in subsection (4):

(a) a buyer who fails to comply with the requirements of Section 6-104(1)(e) with respect to a creditor is liable to the creditor for damages in the amount of the claim, reduced by any amount that the creditor would not have realized if the buyer had complied; and

(b) a buyer who fails to comply with the requirements of any other subsection of Section 6-104 with respect to a claimant is liable to the claimant for damages in the amount of the claim, reduced by any amount that the claimant would not have realized if the buyer had complied.

(2) In an action under subsection (1), the creditor has the burden of establishing the validity and amount of the claim, and the buyer has the burden of establishing the amount that the creditor would not have realized if the buyer had complied.

APPENDIX 8:

APPLICABLE SECTIONS -
UCC ARTICLE 7 - WAREHOUSE RECEIPTS, BILLS OF LADING AND OTHER DOCUMENTS OF TITLE

SECTION 7-201. WHO MAY ISSUE A WAREHOUSE RECEIPT

(1) A warehouse receipt may be issued by any warehouseman.

SECTION 7-202. FORM OF WAREHOUSE RECEIPT; ESSENTIAL TERMS; OPTIONAL TERMS

(1) A warehouse receipt need not be in any particular form.

(2) Unless a warehouse receipt embodies within its written or printed terms each of the following, the warehouseman is liable for damages caused by the omission to a person injured thereby:

(a) the location of the warehouse where the goods are stored;

(b) the date of issue of the receipt;

(c) the consecutive number of the receipt;

(d) a statement whether the goods received will be delivered to the bearer, to a specified person, or to a specified person or his order;

(e) the rate of storage and handling charges, except that where goods are stored under a field warehousing arrangement a statement of that fact is sufficient on a non-negotiable receipt;

(f) a description of the goods or of the packages containing them;

(g) the signature of the warehouseman, which may be made by his authorized agent;

(h) if the receipt is issued for goods of which the warehouseman is owner, either solely or jointly or in common with others, the fact of such ownership; and

(i) a statement of the amount of advances made and of liabilities incurred for which the warehouseman claims a lien or security interest (Section 7-209). If the precise amount of such advances made or of such liabilities incurred is, at the time of the issue of the receipt, unknown to the warehouseman or to his agent who issues it, a statement of the fact that advances have been made or liabilities incurred and the purpose thereof is sufficient.

SECTION 7-204. DUTY OF CARE; CONTRACTUAL LIMITATION OF WAREHOUSEMAN'S LIABILITY

(1) A warehouseman is liable for damages for loss of or injury to the goods caused by his failure to exercise such care in regard to them as a reasonably careful man would exercise under like circumstances but unless otherwise agreed he is not liable for damages which could not have been avoided by the exercise of such care.

(2) Damages may be limited by a term in the warehouse receipt or storage agreement limiting the amount of liability in case of loss or damage, and setting forth a specific liability per article or item, or value per unit of weight, beyond which the warehouseman shall not be liable; provided, however, that such liability may on written request of the bailor at the time of signing such storage agreement or within a reasonable time after receipt of the warehouse receipt be increased on part or all of the goods thereunder, in which event increased rates may be charged based on such increased valuation, but that no such increase shall be permitted contrary to a lawful limitation of liability contained in the warehouseman's tariff, if any. No such limitation is effective with respect to the warehouseman's liability for conversion to his own use.

SECTION 7-206. TERMINATION OF STORAGE AT WAREHOUSEMAN'S OPTION

(1) A warehouseman may on notifying the person on whose account the goods are held and any other person known to claim an interest in the goods require payment of any charges and removal of the goods from the warehouse at the termination of the period of storage fixed by the document, or, if no period is fixed, within a stated period not less than thirty days after the notification. If the goods are not removed before the date specified in the notification, the warehouseman may sell them in accordance with the provisions of the section on enforcement of a warehouseman's lien (Section 7-210).

SECTION 7-209. LIEN OF WAREHOUSEMAN

(1) A warehouseman has a lien against the bailor on the goods covered by a warehouse receipt or on the proceeds thereof in his possession for charges for storage or transportation (including demurrage and terminal charges), insurance, labor, or charges present or future in relation to the goods, and for expenses necessary for preservation of the goods or reasonably incurred in their sale pursuant to law. If the person on whose account the goods are held

is liable for like charges or expenses in relation to other goods whenever deposited and it is stated in the receipt that a lien is claimed for charges and expenses in relation to other goods, the warehouseman also has a lien against him for such charges and expenses whether or not the other goods have been delivered by the warehouseman. But against a person to whom a negotiable warehouse receipt is duly negotiated a warehouseman's lien is limited to charges in an amount or at a rate specified on the receipt or if no charges are so specified then to a reasonable charge for storage of the goods covered by the receipt subsequent to the date of the receipt.

(4) A warehouseman loses his lien on any goods which he voluntarily delivers or which he unjustifiably refuses to deliver.

SECTION 7-210. ENFORCEMENT OF WAREHOUSEMAN'S LIEN

(1) Except as provided in subsection (2), a warehouseman's lien may be enforced by public or private sale of the goods in block or in parcels, at any time or place and on any terms which are commercially reasonable, after notifying all persons known to claim an interest in the goods. Such notification must include a statement of the amount due, the nature of the proposed sale and the time and place of any public sale. The fact that a better price could have been obtained by a sale at a different time or in a different method from that selected by the warehouseman is not of itself sufficient to establish that the sale was not made in a commercially reasonable manner. If the warehouseman either sells the goods in the usual manner in any recognized market therefor, or if he sells at the price current in such market at the time of his sale, or if he has otherwise sold in conformity with commercially reasonable practices among dealers in the type of goods sold, he has sold in a commercially reasonable manner. A sale of more goods than apparently necessary to be offered to insure satisfaction of the obligation is not commercially reasonable except in cases covered by the preceding sentence.

SECTION 7-309. DUTY OF CARE; CONTRACTUAL LIMITATION OF CARRIER'S LIABILITY

(1) A carrier who issues a bill of lading whether negotiable or non-negotiable must exercise the degree of care in relation to the goods which a reasonably careful man would exercise under like circumstances. This subsection does not repeal or change any law or rule of law which imposes liability upon a common carrier for damages not caused by its negligence.

(2) Damages may be limited by a provision that the carrier's liability shall not exceed a value stated in the document if the carrier's rates are dependent upon value and the consignor by the carrier's tariff is afforded an opportunity to declare a higher value or a value as lawfully provided in the tariff, or where no tariff is filed he is otherwise advised of such opportunity; but no such limitation is effective with respect to the carrier's liability for conversion to its own use.

SECTION 7-404. NO LIABILITY FOR GOOD FAITH DELIVERY PURSUANT TO RECEIPT OR BILL

A bailee who in good faith including observance of reasonable commercial standards has received goods and delivered or otherwise disposed of them according to the terms of the document of title or pursuant to this Article is not liable therefor. This rule applies even though the person from whom he received the goods had no authority to procure the document or to dispose of the goods and even though the person to whom he delivered the goods had no authority to receive them.

SECTION 7-507. WARRANTIES ON NEGOTIATION OR TRANSFER OF RECEIPT OR BILL

Where a person negotiates or transfers a document of title for value otherwise than as a mere intermediary under the next following section, then unless otherwise agreed he warrants to his immediate purchaser only in addition to any warranty made in selling the goods

(a) that the document is genuine; and

(b) that he has no knowledge of any fact which would impair its validity or worth; and

(c) that his negotiation or transfer is rightful and fully effective with respect to the title to the document and the goods it represents.

SECTION 7-601. LOST AND MISSING DOCUMENTS

(1) If a document has been lost, stolen or destroyed, a court may order delivery of the goods or issuance of a substitute document and the bailee may without liability to any person comply with such order. If the document was negotiable the claimant must post security approved by the court to indemnify any person who may suffer loss as a result of non-surrender of the document. If the document was not negotiable, such security may be required at the discretion of the court. The court may also in its discretion order payment of the bailee's reasonable costs and counsel fees.

(2) A bailee who without court order delivers goods to a person claiming under a missing negotiable document is liable to any person injured thereby, and if the delivery is not in good faith becomes liable for conversion. Delivery in good faith is not conversion if made in accordance with a filed classification or tariff or, where no classification or tariff is filed, if the claimant posts security with the bailee in an amount at least double the value of the goods at the time of posting to indemnify any person injured by the delivery who files a notice of claim within one year after the delivery.

APPENDIX 9:

APPLICABLE SECTIONS -
UCC ARTICLE 8 - INVESTMENT SECURITIES

SECTION 8-313. WHEN TRANSFER TO PURCHASER OCCURS; FINANCIAL INTERMEDIARY AS BONA FIDE PURCHASER; FINANCIAL INTERMEDIARY

(1) Transfer of a security or a limited interest (including a security interest) therein to a purchaser occurs only:

(a) at the time he or a person designated by him acquires possession of a certificated security;

(b) at the time the transfer, pledge, or release of an uncertificated security is registered to him or a person designated by him;

(c) at the time his financial intermediary acquires possession of a certificated security specially indorsed to or issued in the name of the purchaser;

(d) at the time a financial intermediary, not a clearing corporation, sends him confirmation of the purchase and also by book entry or otherwise identifies as belonging to the purchaser

(i) a specific certificated security in the financial intermediary's possession;

(ii) a quantity of securities that constitute or are part of a fungible bulk of certificated securities in the financial intermediary's possession or of uncertificated securities registered in the name of the financial intermediary; or

(iii) a quantity of securities that constitute or are part of a fungible bulk of securities shown on the account of the financial intermediary on the books of another financial intermediary;

(e) with respect to an identified certificated security to be delivered while still in the possession of a third person, not a financial intermediary, at the time that person acknowledges that he holds for the purchaser;

(f) with respect to a specific uncertificated security the pledge or transfer of which has been registered to a third person, not a financial intermediary, at the time that person acknowledges that he holds for the purchaser.

SECTION 8-315. ACTION AGAINST TRANSFEREE BASED UPON WRONGFUL TRANSFER

(1) Any person against whom the transfer of a security is wrongful for any reason, including his incapacity, as against anyone except a bona fide purchaser, may:

(a) reclaim possession of the certificated security wrongfully transferred;

(b) obtain possession of any new certificated security representing all or part of the same rights;

(c) compel the origination of an instruction to transfer to him or a person designated by him an uncertificated security constituting all or part of the same rights; or

(d) have damages.

(2) If the transfer is wrongful because of an unauthorized indorsement of a certificated security, the owner may also reclaim or obtain possession of the security or a new certificated security, even from a bona fide purchaser, if the ineffectiveness of the purported indorsement can be asserted against him under the provisions of this Article on unauthorized indorsements (Section 8-311).

(3) The right to obtain or reclaim possession of a certificated security or to compel the origination of a transfer instruction may be specifically enforced and the transfer of a certificated or uncertificated security enjoined and a certificated security impounded pending the litigation.

SECTION 8-316. PURCHASER'S RIGHT TO REQUISITES FOR REGISTRATION OF TRANSFER, PLEDGE, OR RELEASE ON BOOKS

Unless otherwise agreed, the transferor of a certificated security or the transferor, pledgor, or pledgee of an uncertificated security on due demand must supply his purchaser with any proof of his authority to transfer, pledge, or release or with any other requisite necessary to obtain registration of the transfer, pledge, or release of the security; but if the transfer, pledge, or release is not for value, a transferor, pledgor, or pledgee need not do so unless the purchaser furnishes the necessary expenses. Failure within a reasonable time to comply with a demand made gives the purchaser the right to reject or rescind the transfer, pledge, or release.

SECTION 8-319. STATUTE OF FRAUDS.

A contract for the sale of securities is not enforceable by way of action or defense unless:

(a) there is some writing signed by the party against whom enforcement is sought or by his authorized agent or broker, sufficient to indicate that a contract has been made for sale of a stated quantity of described securities at a defined or stated price;

(b) delivery of a certificated security or transfer instruction has been accepted, or transfer of an uncertificated security has been registered and the transferee has failed to send written objection to the issuer within 10 days after receipt of the initial transaction statement confirming the registration, or payment has been made, but the contract is enforceable under this provision only to the extent of the delivery, registration, or payment;

(c) within a reasonable time a writing in confirmation of the sale or purchase and sufficient against the sender under paragraph (a) has been received by the party against whom enforcement is sought and he has failed to send written objection to its contents within 10 days after its receipt; or

(d) the party against whom enforcement is sought admits in his pleading, testimony, or otherwise in court that a contract was made for the sale of a stated quantity of described securities at a defined or stated price.

APPLICABLE SECTIONS -
UCC ARTICLE 9 -SECURED TRANSACTIONS

SECTION 9-102. POLICY AND SUBJECT MATTER OF ARTICLE

(1) Except as otherwise provided in Section 9-104 on excluded transactions, this Article applies

(a) to any transaction (regardless of its form) which is intended to create a security interest in personal property or fixtures including goods, documents, instruments, general intangibles, chattel paper or accounts; and also

(b) to any sale of accounts or chattel paper.

(2) This Article applies to security interests created by contract including pledge, assignment, chattel mortgage, chattel trust, trust deed, factor's lien, equipment trust, conditional sale, trust receipt, other lien or title retention contract and lease or consignment intended as security. This Article does not apply to statutory liens except as provided in Section 9-310.

SECTION 9-104. TRANSACTIONS EXCLUDED FROM ARTICLE

This Article does not apply

(a) to a security interest subject to any statute of the United States, to the extent that such statute governs the rights of parties to and third parties affected by transactions in particular types of property; or

(b) to a landlord's lien; or

(c) to a lien given by statute or other rule of law for services or materials except as provided in Section 9-310 on priority of such liens; or

(d) to a transfer of a claim for wages, salary or other compensation of an employee; or

(e) to a transfer by a government or governmental subdivision or agency; or

(f) to a sale of accounts or chattel paper as part of a sale of the business out of which they arose, or an assignment of accounts or chattel paper which is for the purpose of collection only, or a transfer of a right to payment under a contract to an assignee who is also to do the performance under the contract or a transfer of a single account to an assignee in whole or partial satisfaction of a preexisting indebtedness; or

(g) to a transfer of an interest in or claim in or under any policy of insurance, except as provided with respect to proceeds (Section 9-306) and priorities in proceeds (Section 9-312); or

(h) to a right represented by a judgment (other than a judgment taken on a right to payment which was collateral); or

(i) to any right of set-off; or

(j) except to the extent that provision is made for fixtures in Section 9-313, to the creation or transfer of an interest in or lien on real estate, including a lease or rents thereunder; or

(k) to a transfer in whole or in part of any claim arising out of tort; or

(l) to a transfer of an interest in any deposit account (subsection (1) of Section 9-105), except as provided with respect to proceeds (Section 9-306) and priorities in proceeds (Section 9-312).

SECTION 9-112. WHERE COLLATERAL IS NOT OWNED BY DEBTOR

Unless otherwise agreed, when a secured party knows that collateral is owned by a person who is not the debtor, the owner of the collateral is entitled to receive from the secured party any surplus under Section 9-502(2) or under Section 9-504(1), and is not liable for the debt or for any deficiency after resale, and he has the same right as the debtor

(a) to receive statements under Section 9-208;

(b) to receive notice of and to object to a secured party's proposal to retain the collateral in satisfaction of the indebtedness under Section 9-505;

(c) to redeem the collateral under Section 9-506;

(d) to obtain injunctive or other relief under Section 9-507(1); and

(e) to recover losses caused to him under Section 9-208(2).

SECTION 9-203. ATTACHMENT AND ENFORCEABILITY OF SECURITY INTEREST; PROCEEDS; FORMAL REQUISITES

(1) Subject to the provisions of Section 4-208 on the security interest of a collecting bank, Section 8-321 on security interests in securities and Section 9-113 on a security interest arising under the Article on Sales, a security interest is not enforceable against the debtor or third parties with respect to the collateral and does not attach unless:

(a) the collateral is in the possession of the secured party pursuant to agreement, or the debtor has signed a security agreement which contains a description of the collateral and in addition, when the security interest covers crops growing or to be grown or timber to be cut, a description of the land concerned;

(b) value has been given; and

(c) the debtor has rights in the collateral.

SECTION 9-207. RIGHTS AND DUTIES WHEN COLLATERAL IS IN SECURED PARTY'S POSSESSION

(1) A secured party must use reasonable care in the custody and preservation of collateral in his possession. In the case of an instrument or chattel paper reasonable care includes taking necessary steps to preserve rights against prior parties unless otherwise agreed.

(2) Unless otherwise agreed, when collateral is in the secured party's possession

(a) reasonable expenses (including the cost of any insurance and payment of taxes or other charges) incurred in the custody, preservation, use or operation of the collateral are chargeable to the debtor and are secured by the collateral;

(b) the risk of accidental loss or damage is on the debtor to the extent of any deficiency in any effective insurance coverage;

(c) the secured party may hold as additional security any increase or profits (except money) received from the collateral, but money so received, unless remitted to the debtor, shall be applied in reduction of the secured obligation;

(d) the secured party must keep the collateral identifiable but fungible collateral may be commingled;

(e) the secured party may repledge the collateral upon terms which do not impair the debtor's right to redeem it.

(3) A secured party is liable for any loss caused by his failure to meet any obligation imposed by the preceding subsections but does not lose his security interest.

(4) A secured party may use or operate the collateral for the purpose of preserving the collateral or its value or pursuant to the order of a court of appropriate jurisdiction or, except in the case of consumer goods, in the manner and to the extent provided in the security agreement.

SECTION 9-302. WHEN FILING IS REQUIRED TO PERFECT SECURITY INTEREST; SECURITY INTERESTS TO WHICH FILING PROVISIONS OF THIS ARTICLE DO NOT APPLY

(1) A financing statement must be filed to perfect all security interests except the following:

(a) a security interest in collateral in possession of the secured party under Section 9-305;

(b) a security interest temporarily perfected in instruments or documents without delivery under Section 9-304 or in proceeds for a 10 day period under Section 9-306;

(c) a security interest created by an assignment of a beneficial interest in a trust or a decedent's estate;

(d) a purchase money security interest in consumer goods; but filing is required for a motor vehicle required to be registered; and fixture filing is required for priority over conflicting interests in fixtures to the extent provided in Section 9-313;

(e) an assignment of accounts which does not alone or in conjunction with other assignments to the same assignee transfer a significant part of the outstanding accounts of the assignor;

(f) a security interest of a collecting bank (Section 4-208) or in securities (Section 8-321) or arising under the Article on Sales (see Section 9-113) or covered in subsection (3) of this section;

(g) an assignment for the benefit of all the creditors of the transferor, and subsequent transfers by the assignee thereunder.

(2) If a secured party assigns a perfected security interest, no filing under this Article is required in order to continue the perfected status of the security interest against creditors of and transferees from the original debtor.

(3) The filing of a financing statement otherwise required by this Article is not necessary or effective to perfect a security interest in property subject to

(a) a statute or treaty of the United States which provides for a national or international registration or a national or international certificate of title or which specifies a place of filing different from that specified in this Article for filing of the security interest; or

(b) the following statutes of this state; [list any certificate of title statute covering automobiles, trailers, mobile homes, boats, farm tractors, or the like, and any central filing statute .]; but during any period in which collateral is inventory held for sale by a person who is in the business of selling goods of that kind, the filing provisions of this Article (Part 4) apply to a security interest in that collateral created by him as debtor; or

(c) a certificate of title statute of another jurisdiction under the law of which indication of a security interest on the certificate is required as a condition of perfection (subsection (2) of Section 9-103).

(4) Compliance with a statute or treaty described in subsection (3) is equivalent to the filing of a financing statement under this Article, and a security interest in property subject to the statute or treaty can be perfected only by compliance therewith except as provided in Section 9-103 on multiple state transactions. Duration and renewal of perfection of a security interest perfected by compliance with the statute or treaty are governed by the provisions of the statute or treaty; in other respects the security interest is subject to this Article.

SECTION 9-304. PERFECTION OF SECURITY INTEREST IN INSTRUMENTS, DOCUMENTS, AND GOODS COVERED BY DOCUMENTS; PERFECTION BY PERMISSIVE FILING; TEMPORARY PERFECTION WITHOUT FILING OR TRANSFER OF POSSESSION

(1) A security interest in chattel paper or negotiable documents may be perfected by filing. A security interest in money or instruments (other than certificated securities or instruments which constitute part of chattel paper) can be perfected only by the secured party's taking possession, except as provided in subsections (4) and (5) of this section and subsections (2) and (3) of Section 9-306 on proceeds.

(2) During the period that goods are in the possession of the issuer of a negotiable document therefor, a security interest in the goods is perfected by perfecting a security interest in the document, and any security interest in the goods otherwise perfected during such period is subject thereto.

(3) A security interest in goods in the possession of a bailee other than one who has issued a negotiable document therefor is perfected by issuance of a document in the name of the secured party or by the bailee's receipt of notification of the secured party's interest or by filing as to the goods.

(4) A security interest in instruments (other than certificated securities) or negotiable documents is perfected without filing or the taking of possession for a period of 21 days from the time it attaches to the extent that it arises for new value given under a written security agreement.

(5) A security interest remains perfected for a period of 21 days without filing where a secured party having a perfected security interest in an instrument (other than a certificated security), a negotiable document or goods in possession of a bailee other than one who has issued a negotiable document therefor

   (a) makes available to the debtor the goods or documents representing the goods for the purpose of ultimate sale or exchange or for the purpose of loading, unloading, storing, shipping, transshipping, manufacturing, processing or otherwise dealing with them in a manner preliminary to their sale or exchange, but priority between conflicting security interests in the goods is subject to subsection (3) of Section 9-312; or

   (b) delivers the instrument to the debtor for the purpose of ultimate sale or exchange or of presentation, collection, renewal or registration of transfer.

(6) After the 21 day period in subsections (4) and (5) perfection depends upon compliance with applicable provisions of this Article.

SECTION 9-305. WHEN POSSESSION BY SECURED PARTY PERFECTS SECURITY INTEREST WITHOUT FILING

A security interest in letters of credit and advices of credit (subsection (2)(a) of Section 5-116), goods, instruments (other than certificated securities), money, negotiable documents, or chattel paper may be perfected by the secured party's taking possession of the collateral. If such collateral other than goods covered by a negotiable document is held by a bailee, the secured party is deemed to have possession from the time the bailee receives notification of the secured party's interest. A security interest is perfected by possession from the time possession is taken without a relation back and continues only so long as possession is retained, unless otherwise specified in this Article. The security interest may be otherwise perfected as provided in this Article before or after the period of possession by the secured party.

SECTION 9-402. FORMAL REQUISITES OF FINANCING STATEMENT; AMENDMENTS; MORTGAGE AS FINANCING STATEMENT

(1) A financing statement is sufficient if it gives the names of the debtor and the secured party, is signed by the debtor, gives an address of the secured party from which information concerning the security interest may be obtained, gives a mailing address of the debtor and contains a statement indicating the types, or describing the items, of collateral. A financing statement

may be filed before a security agreement is made or a security interest otherwise attaches. When the financing statement covers crops growing or to be grown, the statement must also contain a description of the real estate concerned. When the financing statement covers timber to be cut or covers minerals or the like (including oil and gas) or accounts subject to subsection (5) of Section 9-103, or when the financing statement is filed as a fixture filing (Section 9-313) and the collateral is goods which are or are to become fixtures, the statement must also comply with subsection (5). A copy of the security agreement is sufficient as a financing statement if it contains the above information and is signed by the debtor. A carbon, photographic or other reproduction of a security agreement or a financing statement is sufficient as a financing statement if the security agreement so provides or if the original has been filed in this state.

(2) A financing statement which otherwise complies with subsection (1) is sufficient when it is signed by the secured party instead of the debtor if it is filed to perfect a security interest in

(a) collateral already subject to a security interest in another jurisdiction when it is brought into this state, or when the debtor's location is changed to this state. Such a financing statement must state that the collateral was brought into this state or that the debtor's location was changed to this state under such circumstances; or

(b) proceeds under Section 9-306 if the security interest in the original collateral was perfected. Such a financing statement must describe the original collateral; or

(c) collateral as to which the filing has lapsed; or

(d) collateral acquired after a change of name, identity or corporate structure of the debtor (subsection (7)).

SECTION 9-406. RELEASE OF COLLATERAL

A secured party of record may by his signed statement release all or a part of any collateral described in a filed financing statement. The statement of release is sufficient if it contains a description of the collateral being released, the name and address of the debtor, the name and address of the secured party, and the file number of the financing statement . . .

SECTION 9-501. DEFAULT; PROCEDURE WHEN SECURITY AGREEMENT COVERS BOTH REAL AND PERSONAL PROPERTY

(1) When a debtor is in default under a security agreement, a secured party has the rights and remedies provided in this Part and except as limited by subsection (3) those provided in the security agreement. He may reduce his claim to judgment, foreclose or otherwise enforce the security interest by any available judicial procedure. If the collateral is documents the secured party may proceed either as to the documents or as to the goods covered thereby. A secured party in possession has the rights, remedies and duties provided in Section 9-207. The rights and remedies referred to in this subsection are cumulative.

(2) After default, the debtor has the rights and remedies provided in this Part, those provided in the security agreement and those provided in Section 9-207.

(3) To the extent that they give rights to the debtor and impose duties on the secured party, the rules stated in the subsections referred to below may not be waived or varied except as provided with respect to compulsory disposition of collateral (subsection (3) of Section 9-504 and Section 9-505) and with respect to redemption of collateral (Section 9-506) but the parties may by agreement determine the standards by which the fulfillment of these rights and duties is to be measured if such standards are not manifestly unreasonable:

(a) subsection (2) of Section 9-502 and subsection (2) of Section 9-504 insofar as they require accounting for surplus proceeds of collateral;

(b) subsection (3) of Section 9-504 and subsection (1) of Section 9-505 which deal with disposition of collateral;

(c) subsection (2) of Section 9-505 which deals with acceptance of collateral as discharge of obligation;

(d) Section 9-506 which deals with redemption of collateral; and

(e) subsection (1) of Section 9-507 which deals with the secured party's liability for failure to comply with this Part.

(4) If the security agreement covers both real and personal property, the secured party may proceed under this Part as to the personal property or he may proceed as to both the real and the personal property in accordance with his rights and remedies in respect of the real property in which case the provisions of this Part do not apply.

(5) When a secured party has reduced his claim to judgment the lien of any levy which may be made upon his collateral by virtue of any execution based upon the judgment shall relate back to the date of the perfection of the security interest in such collateral. A judicial sale, pursuant to such execution, is a foreclosure of the security interest by judicial procedure within the meaning of this section, and the secured party may purchase at the sale and thereafter hold the collateral free of any other requirements of this Article.

GLOSSARY

GLOSSARY

Acceleration Clause - A provision or clause in a contract or document establishing that upon the occurrence of a certain event, such as a default in payments, a party's expected interest in the subject property will become prematurely vested.

Acceptance - Refers to one's consent to the terms of an offer, which consent creates a contract.

Acceptor - A drawee who has accepted a draft.

Accord and Satisfaction - Refers to the payment of money, or other thing of value, which is usually less than the amount owed or demanded, in exchange for extinguishment of the debt.

Account - Any deposit or credit account with a bank , including a demand, time, savings, passbook, share draft, or like account , other than an account evidenced by a certificate of deposit.

Account Debtor - With respect to secured transactions, means the person who is obligated on an account, chattel paper or general intangible.

Action - In the sense of a judicial proceeding, includes recoupment, counterclaim, set-off, suit in equity and any other proceedings in which rights are determined.

Actual Damages - Refers to those damages directly referable to the breach or tortious act and which can be readily proven to have been sustained and for which the injured party should be compensated as a matter of right. Also referred to as compensatory or general damages.

Adhesion Contract - A standardized contract form offered to consumers of goods and services on a "take it or leave it" basis without affording the consumer a realistic opportunity to bargain, and under such conditions that the consumer cannot obtain the desired product or service except by acquiescing in form contract.

Agency - The relationship in which one person acts for or represents another by the latter's authority, such as principal and agent or proprietor and independent contractor relationships.

Agent - One who represents and acts for another under the contract or relation of agency.

Aggrieved Party - A party entitled to resort to a remedy.

Agreement - The bargain of the parties in fact as found in their language or by implication from other circumstances including course of dealing or usage of trade or course of performance as provided in UCC Sections 1-205 and 1-206.

Airbill - A document serving for air transportation as a bill of lading does for marine or rail transportation, and includes an air consignment note or air waybill.

Amortization Schedule - A plan for the payment of an indebtedness where there are partial payments of the principal and accrued interest, at stated periods for a definite time, upon the expiration of which the entire indebtedness will be extinguished.

Annual Percentage Rate (APR) - The actual cost of borrowing money, expressed in the form of an annual rate to make it easy for one to compare the cost of borrowing money among several lenders.

Anticipatory Breach - A breach committed prior to the actual time of required performance which occurs when one party by declaration repudiates his contractual obligation before it is due.

Apparent Agency - Refers to the situation when one person, whether or not authorized, reasonably appears to a third person, due to the manifestation of another, to be authorized to act as agent for such other.

Assets - With respect to bulk sales, the inventory that is the subject of a bulk sale and any tangible and intangible personal property used or held for use primarily in, or arising from, the seller's business and sold in connection with that inventory.

Attorney in Fact - An agent or representative of another given authority to act in that person's name and place pursuant to a document called a "power of attorney."

Bailee - The person who by a warehouse receipt, bill of lading or other document of title acknowledges possession of goods and contracts to deliver them.

Bank - A person engaged in the business of banking and includes a savings bank, savings and loan association, credit union, and trust company.

Banking Day - The part of a day on which a bank is open to the public for carrying on substantially all of its banking functions.

Bankrupt - The state or condition of one who is unable to pay his debts as they are, or become, due.

Bankruptcy - The legal process under federal law intended to insure fairness and equality among creditors of a bankrupt person, also known as a debtor, and to enable the debtor to start fresh by retaining certain property exempt from liabilities and unhampered by preexisting debts.

Bearer - The person in possession of an instrument, document of title, or certificated security payable to bearer or indorsed in blank.

Bilateral Contract - A contract containing mutual promises between the parties to the contract, each being termed both a promisor and a promisee.

Bill of Lading - A document evidencing the receipt of goods for shipment issued by a person engaged in the business of transporting or forwarding goods, including an airbill.

Boilerplate - Refers to the standard or formal language found in legal documents of a given type, often in small print.

Breach of Contract - The failure, without any legal excuse, to perform any promise which forms the whole or the part of a contract.

Broker - With respect to investment securities, means a person defined as a broker or dealer under the federal securities laws, without excluding a bank acting in that capacity.

Bulk Sale - In the case of (i) a sale by auction or a sale or series of sales conducted by a liquidator on the seller's behalf, a sale or series of sales not in the ordinary course of the seller's business of more than half of the seller's inventory, as measured by value on the date of the bulk-sale agreement, if on that date the auctioneer or liquidator has notice, or after reasonable inquiry would have had notice, that the seller will not continue to operate the same or a similar kind of business after the sale or series of sales; and in all other cases (ii) a sale not in the ordinary course of the seller's business of more than half the seller's inventory, as measured by value on the date of the bulk-sale agreement, if on that date the buyer has notice, or after reasonable inquiry would have had notice, that the seller will not continue to operate the same or a similar kind of business after the sale.

Burden of Establishing a Fact - The burden of persuading the triers of fact that the existence of the fact is more probable than its non-existence.

Buyer - A person who buys or contracts to buy goods.

Buyer in Ordinary Course of Business - A person who in good faith and without knowledge that the sale to him is in violation of the ownership rights or security interest of a third party in the goods buys in ordinary course from a person in the business of selling goods of that kind, not including a pawnbroker.

Cancellation - Occurs when either party puts an end to the contract for breach by the other and its effect is the same as that of termination, except that the canceling party also retains any remedy for breach of the whole contract or any unperformed balance.

Capacity - The legal qualification concerning the ability of one to understand the nature and effects of one's acts.

Certificated Security - A security that is represented by a certificate.

Chattel Paper - A writing which evidences both a monetary obligation and a security interest in or a lease of specific goods.

Clearing Corporation - With respect to investment securities, generally refers to a person that is registered as a clearing agency under the federal securities laws; a federal reserve bank; or any other person that provides clearance or settlement services with respect to financial assets.

Clearinghouse - An association of banks or other payors regularly clearing items.

Collateral - Property which is pledged as security for the satisfaction of a debt.

Commercial Unit - A unit of goods that, by commercial usage, is a single whole for purposes of sale, and division of which materially impairs its character or value on the market or in use. May be a single article, a set of articles, or a quantity or any other unit treated in use or in the relevant market as a single whole.

Common Law - The system of jurisprudence which originated in England and was later applied in the United States. The common law is based on judicial precedent rather than statutory law.

Compensatory Damages - Refers to those damages directly referable to the breach or tortious act and which can be readily proven to have been sustained and for which the injured party should be compensated as a matter of right. Also referred to as actual or general damages.

Condition - A future and uncertain event upon the happening of which is made to depend the existence of an obligation.

Condition Concurrent - Refers to a condition precedent which exists only when parties to a contract are found to render performance at the same time.

Condition Precedent - Refers to a condition which must occur before the agreement becomes effective and which calls for the happening of some event before the contract shall be binding on the parties.

Condition Subsequent - Refers to a provision giving one party the right to divest himself of liability and obligation to perform further if the other party fails to meet the condition.

Conforming Goods or Performance - Under a lease contract, means goods or performance that are in accordance with the obligations contained therein.

Consequential Damages - Refers to those damages which are caused by an injury but which are not a necessary result of the injury and must be specially pleaded and proven in order to be awarded.

Consideration - Something of value given in return for a performance or promise of performance by another, for the purpose of forming a contract.

Consignee - The person named in a bill to whom or to whose order the bill promises delivery.

Consignor - The person named in a bill as the person from whom the goods have been received for shipment.

Conspicuous - A term or clause is conspicuous when it is written so that a reasonable person against whom it is to operate ought to have noticed it.

Consumer lease - A lease that a lessor regularly engaged in the business of leasing or selling makes to a lessee who is an individual and who takes under the lease primarily for a personal, family, or household purpose.

Contract - A contract is an agreement between two or more persons which creates an obligation to do or not to do a particular thing.

Counteroffer - A statement by the offeree which has the legal effect of rejecting the offer and of proposing a new offer to the offeror.

Credit - Credit is that which is extended to the buyer or borrower on the seller or lender's belief that that which is given will be repaid.

Credit Report - The document issued by a credit reporting agency setting forth a credit rating and pertinent financial data concerning a person or a company, which is used by banks, lenders, merchants, and suppliers in evaluating a credit risk.

Customer - With respect to a bank, means a person, including a bank, having an account with a bank or from whom a bank has agreed to receive payment orders.

Damages - In general, damages refers to monetary compensation which the law awards to one who has been injured by the actions of another, such as in the case of tortious conduct or breach of contractual obligations.

Default - A failure to discharge a duty or do that which ought to be done.

Delivery - With respect to instruments, documents of title, chattel paper, or certificated securities means voluntary transfer of possession.

Delivery Order - A written order to deliver goods directed to a warehouseman, carrier or other person who in the ordinary course of business issues warehouse receipts or bills of lading.

Deposit Account - A demand, time, savings, passbook or like account maintained with a bank, savings and loan association, credit union or like organization, other than an account evidenced by a certificate of deposit.

Disclosure - The act of disclosing or revealing that which is secret or not fully understood. The Truth in Lending Act provides that there be disclosure to the consumer of certain information deemed basic to an intelligent assessment of a credit transaction.

Discount Rate - The percentage of the face amount of commercial paper which a holder pays when he transfers such paper to a financial institution for cash or credit.

Documentary Draft - A draft to be presented for acceptance or payment if specified documents, certificated securities, instructions for uncertificated securities, or other certificates, statements, or the like are to be received by the drawee or other payor before acceptance or payment of the draft.

Document of Title - A bill of lading, dock warrant, dock receipt, warehouse receipt or order for the delivery of goods, including any other document which in the regular course of business or financing is treated as adequately evidencing that the person in possession of it is entitled to receive, hold and dispose of the document and the goods it covers.

Drawee - A person ordered in a draft to make payment.

Duress - Refers to action by one person which propels another person to do something he or she would not otherwise do.

Encumbrance - A real estate mortgage or other lien on real estate and all other rights in real estate that are not ownership interests.

Entitlement Holder - A person identified in the records of a securities intermediary as the person having a security entitlement against the securities intermediary.

Entitlement Order - A notification communicated to a securities intermediary directing transfer or redemption of a financial asset to which the entitlement holder has a security entitlement.

Excuse - A matter alleged as a reason for relief or exemption from some duty or obligation.

Fault - A wrongful act, omission, breach or default.

Federal Trade Commission - An agency of the federal government created in 1914 for the purpose of promoting free and fair competition in interstate commerce through the prevention of general trade restraints such as price-fixing agreements, false advertising, boycotts, illegal combinations of competitors and other unfair methods of competition.

Finance Charge - Any charge assessed for an extension of credit, including interest.

Financing Agency - A bank, finance company or other person who in the ordinary course of business makes advances against goods or documents of title or who by arrangement with either the seller or the buyer intervenes in ordinary course to make or collect payment due or claimed under the contract for sale. Includes also a bank or other person who similarly intervenes between persons who are in the position of seller and buyer in respect to the goods.

Fraud - A false representation of a matter of fact, whether by words or by conduct, by false or misleading allegations, or by concealment of that which should have been disclosed, which deceives and is intended to deceive another so that he shall act upon it to his legal injury.

Free on Board (FOB) - A commercial term that signifies a contractual agreement between a buyer and a seller to have the subject of a sale delivered to a designated place, usually either the place of shipment or the place of destination, without expense to the buyer.

Frustration of Purpose - Frustration of purpose in contract law occurs when an implied condition of an agreement does not occur or ceases to exist without fault of either party such that the absence of the implied condition frustrates one party intentions in making the agreement.

Funds Transfer - The series of transactions, beginning with the originator's payment order, made for the purpose of making payment to the beneficiary of the order.

Funds-Transfer Business Day - The part of a day during which a receiving bank is open for the receipt, processing, and transmittal of payment orders and cancellations and amendments of payment orders.

Funds-Transfer System - A wire transfer network, automated clearinghouse, or other communication system of a clearinghouse or other association of banks through which a payment order by a bank may be transmitted to the bank to which the order is addressed.

Fungible - With respect to goods or securities, means goods or securities of which any unit is, by nature or usage of trade, the equivalent of any other like unit. Goods which are not fungible shall be deemed fungible for the purposes of the UCC to the extent that under a particular agreement or document unlike units are treated as equivalents.

General Damages - Refers to those damages directly referable to the breach or tortious act and which can be readily proven to have been sustained and for which the injured party should be compensated as a matter of right. Also referred to as actual or compensatory damages.

Genuine - Free of forgery or counterfeiting.

Good Faith - In the case of a merchant, means honesty in fact and the observance of reasonable commercial standards of fair dealing in the trade.

Goods - All things which are movable at the time of identification to the contract for sale.

Grace Period - The period beyond the due date set forth in the contract during which time payment may be made without incurring a penalty.

Holder - As it refers to a negotiable instrument, it means the person in possession if the instrument is payable to bearer, or the identified person if such person is in possession. As it refers to a document of title, it means the person in possession if the goods are deliverable to bearer or to the order of the person in possession.

Honor - To pay or to accept and pay.

Impossibility - A defense to breach of contract and arises when performance is impossible due to the destruction of the subject matter of the contract or the death of a person necessary for performance.

Incapacity - A defense to breach of contract which refers to a lack of legal, physical or intellectual power to enter into a contract.

Indemnification Clause - In contract law, refers to the agreement by one party to secure the other party against loss or damage which may occur in the future in connection with performance of the contract.

Indorsement - With respect to investment securities, refers to a signature that alone or accompanied by other words is made on a security certificate in registered form or on a separate document for the purpose of assigning, transferring, or redeeming the security or granting a power to assign, transfer, or redeem it.

Insolvency Proceedings - Any assignment for the benefit of creditors or other proceedings intended to liquidate or rehabilitate the estate of the person involved.

Insolvent - A person who either has ceased to pay his debts in the ordinary course of business or cannot pay his debts as they become due or is insolvent within the meaning of the federal bankruptcy law.

Installment Contract - A contract in which the obligation, such as the payment of money, is divided into a series of successive performances over a period of time.

Installment Lease Contract - A lease contract that authorizes or requires the delivery of goods in separate lots to be separately accepted.

Instruction - With respect to investment securities, refers to a notification communicated to the issuer of an uncertificated security which directs that the transfer of the security be registered or that the security be redeemed.

Instrument - Refers to a negotiable instrument under UCC - Article 3, or a certificated security under UCC - Article 8, or any other writing which evidences a right to the payment of money and is not itself a security agreement or lease and is of a type which is in ordinary course of business transferred by delivery with any necessary indorsement or assignment.

Interest - The compensation paid for the use of money loaned.

Item - With respect to a bank, an instrument, promise or order to pay money handled by a bank for collection or payment.

Joint and Several - The sharing of rights and liabilities among a group of people collectively and individually.

Judgment - A final determination by a court of law concerning the rights of the parties to a lawsuit.

Knowledge - A person has knowledge of a fact when he has actual knowledge of it.

Lease - A transfer of the right to possession and use of goods for a term in return for consideration.

Lease Agreement - The bargain, with respect to the lease, of the lessor and the lessee in fact as found in their language or by implication from other circumstances including course of dealing or usage of trade or course of performance.

Lease Contract - The total legal obligation that results from the lease agreement.

Leasehold Interest - The interest of the lessor or the lessee under a lease contract.

Lessee - A person who acquires the right to possession and use of goods under a lease.

Lessee in Ordinary Course of Business - A person who in good faith and without knowledge that the lease is in violation of the ownership rights or security interest or leasehold interest of a third party in the goods leases in ordinary course from a person in the business of selling or leasing goods of that kind, not including a pawnbroker.

Lessor - A person who transfers the right to possession and use of goods under a lease.

Lessor's Residual Interest - The lessor's interest in the goods after expiration, termination, or cancellation of the lease contract.

Letter of Credit - An engagement by a bank or other person, made at the request of a customer, that the issuer will honor drafts or other demands for payment upon compliance with the conditions specified in the credit.

Liability - Refers to one's obligation to do or refrain from doing something, such as the payment of a debt.

Lien - A charge against or interest in goods to secure payment of a debt or performance of an obligation.

Liquidated Damages - The amount stipulated by the parties to a contract representing a reasonable estimate of the damages which would result from a breach by the parties.

Liquidator - A person who is regularly engaged in the business of disposing of assets for businesses contemplating liquidation or dissolution.

Loan Principal - The amount of the debt not including interest or any other additions.

Lot - A parcel or a single article which is the subject matter of a separate sale or delivery, whether or not it is sufficient to perform the contract.

Maker - A person who signs or is identified in a note as a person undertaking to pay.

Material Breach - A substantial breach of contract which excuses further performance by the innocent party and gives rise to an action for breach of contract by that party.

Merchant - A person who deals in goods of a particular kind, or otherwise by his occupation holds himself out as having knowledge or skill peculiar to the practices or goods involved in the transaction or to whom such knowledge or skill may be attributed by his employment of an agent or broker or other intermediary who by his occupation holds himself out as having such knowledge or skill.

Merchant Lessee - A lessee that is a merchant with respect to goods of the kind subject to the lease.

Merger Clause - A provision in a contract which states that the written terms of the agreement may not be varied by prior or oral agreements because all such agreements are said to have merged into the writing.

Midnight Deadline - With respect to a bank, refers to midnight on its next banking day following the banking day on which it receives the relevant item or notice, or from which the time for taking action commences to run, whichever is later.

Mitigation of Damages - The duty imposed on an injured party to exercise reasonable diligence in attempting to minimize the damages resulting from the injury.

Money - A medium of exchange authorized or adopted by a domestic or foreign government, including a monetary unit of account established by an intergovernmental organization or by agreement between two or more nations.

Mortgage - A consensual interest created by a real estate mortgage, a trust deed on real estate, or the like.

Mutual Agreement - The meeting of the minds of the parties to a contract concerning the subject matter of the contract.

Notice - A person has notice of a fact when (a) he has actual knowledge of it; (b) he has received a notice or notification of it; or (c) from all the facts and circumstances known to him at the time in question he has reason to know that it exists.

Notification - A person gives notification to another by taking such steps as may be reasonably required to inform the other in ordinary course whether or not such other actually comes to know of it.

Novation - The substitution of a new party and the discharge of an original party to a contract, with the assent of all parties.

Offer - A manifestation of willingness to enter into a bargain which invites the acceptance of the person to whom the offer is made.

Offeree - The person to whom an offer is made.

Offeror - The person who makes an offer.

Oral Agreement - An agreement which is not in writing or not signed by the parties.

Order - A written instruction to pay money signed by the person giving the instruction.

Ordinary Care - In the case of a person engaged in business, means observance of reasonable commercial standards, prevailing in the area in which the person is located, with respect to the business in which the person is engaged.

Organization - A corporation, government or governmental subdivision or agency, business trust, estate, trust, partnership or association, two or more persons having a joint or common interest, or any other legal or commercial entity.

Parol Evidence Rule - The doctrine which holds that the written terms of an agreement may not be varied by prior or oral agreements.

Party - As it refers to negotiable instruments, means a party to an instrument.

Payment Order - An instruction of a sender to a receiving bank, transmitted orally, electronically, or in writing, to pay, or to cause another bank to pay, a fixed or determinable amount of money to a beneficiary.

Performance - The completion of one's contractual obligation.

Person - An individual or an organization.

Present Value - The amount as of a date certain of one or more sums payable in the future, discounted to the date certain.

Presumption - Procedure by which the trier of fact must find the existence of the fact presumed unless and until evidence is introduced which would support a finding of its non-existence.

Privity of Contract - The relationship between the parties to a contract.

Promise - A written undertaking to pay money signed by the person undertaking to pay.

Purchase - Taking by sale, lease, mortgage, security interest, pledge, gift, or any other voluntary transaction creating an interest in goods.

Purchase Order - A document which authorizes a seller to deliver goods and is considered an offer which is accepted upon delivery.

Purchaser - A person who takes by purchase.

Quantum Meruit - An equitable doctrine based on unjust enrichment which refers to the extent of liability in a contract implied by law, also known as a quasi-contract, wherein the court infers a reasonable amount payable for goods and services even when there is no contract between the parties.

Quasi-Contract - The legal obligation invoked in the absence of an agreement where there has been unjust enrichment.

Quid Pro Quo - The mutual consideration which passes between the parties to a contract rendering it valid and binding.

Receipt of Goods - Occurs when physical possession is taken of the goods.

Reformation - An equitable remedy which calls for the rewriting of a contract involving a mutual mistake or fraud.

Remedy - The means by which a right is enforced or a violation of a right is compensated.

Remitter - A person who purchases an instrument from its issuer if the instrument is payable to an identified person other than the purchaser.

Repudiation - The refusal by one party to a contract to perform a duty or obligation owed to the other party.

Representative - An agent, an officer of a corporation or association, and a trustee, executor or administrator of an estate, or any other person empowered to act for another.

Rescission - The cancellation of a contract which returns the parties to the positions they were in before the contract was made.

Restatement of Contracts - A series of volumes written and published by the American Law Institute (ALI) which attempts to state an orderly explanation of the current and evolving law of contracts, and sets forth a proposed direction which the ALI believes contract law should follow.

Restitution - The act of restoring a party to a contract to their status quo, i.e., the position the party would have been in if no contract had been made.

Secured Party - A lender, seller or other person in whose favor there is a security interest, including a person to whom accounts or chattel paper have been sold.

Security - Refers to (A) an obligation of an issuer or a share, participation, or other interest in an issuer or in property or an enterprise of an issuer which: (i) is represented by a security certificate in bearer or registered form; (ii) is one of a class or series or by its terms is divisible into a class or series of shares, participations, interests, or obligations; and (iii) is a type, dealt in or traded on securities exchanges or securities markets; or (B) is a medium for investment and by its terms expressly provides that it is a security governed by UCC - Article 8.

Security Agreement - An agreement which creates or provides for a security interest.

Security Certificate - A certificate representing a security.

Security Entitlement - The rights and property interest of an entitlement holder with respect to a financial asset.

Security Interest - An interest in personal property or fixtures which secures payment or performance of an obligation.

Securities Intermediary - Refers to a clearing corporation ; or a person, including a bank or broker, that in the ordinary course of its business maintains securities accounts for others and is acting in that capacity.

Seller - A person who sells or contracts to sell goods.

Send - In connection with any writing or notice means to deposit in the mail or deliver for transmission by any other usual means of communication with postage or cost of transmission provided for and properly addressed.

Settle - With respect to a bank, means to pay in cash, by clearinghouse settlement, in a charge or credit, or by remittance, or otherwise as agreed.

Signed - Any symbol executed or adopted by a party with present intention to authenticate a writing.

Specific Performance - The equitable remedy available to an aggrieved party where there has been a breach of contract which requires the guilty party to perform his or her obligations under the contract.

Statute of Frauds - The requirement that certain contracts must be in writing to be legally enforceable.

Sublease - A lease of goods the right to possession and use of which was acquired by the lessor as a lessee under an existing lease.

Substantial Performance - The performance of all of the essential terms of a contract so that the purpose of the contract has been accomplished giving rise to the right to compensation even though minor omissions may exist.

Supplier - A person from whom a lessor buys or leases goods to be leased under a finance lease.

Supply Contract - A contract under which a lessor buys or leases goods to be leased.

Surety - Guarantor.

Suspend Payments - With respect to a bank, means that it has been closed by order of the supervisory authorities, that a public officer has been appointed to take it over, or that it ceases or refuses to make payments in the ordinary course of business.

Telegram - Refers to a message transmitted by radio, teletype, cable, or any mechanical method of transmission.

Term - That portion of an agreement which relates to a particular matter.

Termination - That which occurs when either party pursuant to a power created by agreement or law puts an end to the contract otherwise than for its breach. On termination, all obligations which are still executory on both sides are discharged but any right based on prior breach or performance survives.

Transmitting Utility - Any person primarily engaged in the railroad, street railway or trolley bus business, the electric or electronics communications transmission business, the transmission of goods by pipeline, or the transmission or the production and transmission of electricity, steam, gas or water, or the provision of sewer service.

Unauthorized Signature - A signature made without actual, implied, or apparent authority, including a forgery.

Uncertificated Security - A security that is not represented by a certificate.

Unconscionable - The condition of a contract which is so one-sided and detrimental to the interest of one of the parties that it operates to render the contract unenforceable.

Uniform Commercial Code (UCC) - A code of laws governing commercial transactions which was drafted by the National Conference of Commissioners on Uniform State Laws and designed to bring uniformity to the laws of the various states.

Unilateral Contract - A contract whereby one party makes a promise to do or refrain from doing something in return for actual performance by the other party.

Usury - An excessive and illegal rate of interest.

Value - With respect to negotiable instruments and bank collections as set forth in UCC Sections 3-303, 4-208 and 4-209, a person gives "value" for rights if he acquires them (a) in return for a binding commitment to extend credit or for the extension of immediately available credit whether or not drawn upon and whether or not a charge-back is provided for in the event of difficulties in collection; (b) as security for or in total or partial satisfaction of a pre-existing claim; (c) by accepting delivery pursuant to a pre-existing contract for purchase; or (d) generally, in return for any consideration sufficient to support a simple contract.

Waiver - An intentional and voluntary surrender of a known right.

Warehouseman - A person engaged in the business of storing goods for hire.

Warehouse Receipt - A receipt issued by a person engaged in the business of storing goods for hire.

BIBLIOGRAPHY

BIBLIOGRAPHY

Black's Law Dictionary, Fifth Edition. St. Paul, MN: West Publishing Company, 1979.

Cornell Law School Legal Information Institute. (Date Visited: September 1998) http://www.law.cornell.edu/.

National Conference of Commissioners on Uniform State Laws - Official Site. (Date Visited: September 1998) http://www.law.upenn.edu/bll/ulc/ulc.htm/.

The Portable UCC. Chicago, IL: American Bar Association Section of Business Law, 1993.

Stone, Bradford, *Uniform Commercial Code, Fourth Edition.* St. Paul, MN: West Publishing Co., 1995.

DATE DUE

FEB 03			
GAYLORD			PRINTED IN U.S.A.